Android Development On Android Studio

El quent roid

Android Development On Android Studio

Eloquent roid

Al-Kathiri Khalid

First Print, September 2016

To Khalis, Khayla and you the reader,

Blessed are they who apply the knowledge they gain, gained knowledge is an applied skill to generate value for indeed knowledge without experience is just information.

Al-Kathiri Khalid.

Special thanks,

I would like to give special thanks to my Mother for granting me the most precious gem of them all and that is Education.

Special thanks also goes to another truly precious gem my wife Naadira for all the love, courage, support and care she has bestowed on me and our kin, may we be blessed through the years to come.

Thank You.

Al-Kathiri Khalid.

Contents

Preface   14

Features   14

About The Author   15

Before You Begin   16

Who Is This Book for?   16

How to Use This Book   16

JDK Installation   16

Java Path Setup   18

Chapter 1   21

Introduction   21

    What is Android   21

    What is Android Studio   21

    System Requirements   21

Installation and Setup   22

    Installing Android Studio   22

    Adding SDK Packages   28

    Android SDK Path Setup   30

    Android Virtual Device   32

    Setup a Virtual Device   34

    Setup a Mobile Device   38

Quick Commands   40

    Android Studio Keyboard Shortcuts   40

    Android Tools and Commands   41

        Android   41

        ADB   42

        Lint   43

Knowledge Check   44

Lab Exercise   45

Chapter 2   46

Introduction   46

    Platform Version and Distribution   46

How to Start Android App Development   48

    Through Android Studio IDE   48

Through Command Line 52

How to Launch Android App 54

    Launch Android App Through Android Studio IDE 54

    Launch Android App Through Command Line 54

Understanding Android App Structure 56

    Folders 56

    Files 56

Analyzing App Source Code 58

    Main Activity Class 58

    Activity Layout 61

    Android Manifest File 64

    Manifest File Structure 66

    Gradle Build File 68

Android Architecture 70

    The Linux Kernel 72

    Hardware Abstraction Layer 72

    Android Runtime 72

    Native C/C++ Libraries 72

    Java API Framework 73

    System Apps 73

Android Activity Lifecycle 74

    onCreate 74

    onStart 74

    onResume 74

    onPause 74

    onStop 74

    onDestroy 75

    onRestart 75

Knowledge Check 80

Lab Exercise 81

Chapter 3 82

Introduction 82

Source Control 82

    Android Studio Version Control 82

Git   84

  Installation and setup   84

  Git Commands   86

  Git installation verification   86

  Android Studio Git Setup   88

Notepad App   90

  Launcher Icon   94

  Impact on View   94

  Impact on Performance   94

  Notepad App Git Setup   96

  Add files to be tracked by Git   98

  List tracked and untracked files by Git   100

Before Developing   102

Planning   104

  Wireframe   104

  User Actions Overall - Empty App   104

  First Screen   104

  Second Screen   104

  User Actions - Unempty App   106

  First Screen   106

  Second Screen   106

  Wireframe Gestures presentation   110

Knowledge Check   112

Lab Exercise   113

Chapter 4   114

Introduction   114

Building Notepad UI   114

  Note Edit   116

  Original   116

  Modified   116

  Explanation   116

  Notes List   118

  Original   118

  Modified   118

Explanation 118

Notes Row 120

Original 120

Modified 120

Explanation 120

Adding a Menu 122

Building Notepad App Backend 130

Notes Db Adapter 132

Note Edit 136

Notepad 138

Manifest 140

Knowledge Check 142

Lab Exercise 143

Chapter 5 144

Introduction 144

Audio Recorder 144

Audio Recorder Design 144

Audio Recorder Build 146

Front End Coding 156

Change the layout 156

Back End Coding 160

Setting a Button 160

Setting File Path 162

Setting MediaRecorder and MediaPlayer 164

Setting Activity Flow 172

Setting AudioRecorder Logic 174

Setting Permission to Record Audio 176

Changing Launcher Icon 178

Make the Application work 182

Launch Audio Record 186

Code Inspection 192

Configuring Lint 192

Running Lint 192

Lint Results 194

Knowledge Check   196

Lab Exercise   197

Chapter 6   198

Introduction   198

Prerelease Preparation   198

   Versioning and Upgrades   198

   Signing and Packaging to APK   200

   Creating Release Key and Signing a release build 202

   Through Android Studio   202

   Through Command line   204

Google Play   206

   Sign Up for a Publisher Account   206

   Merchant Countries   208

   Merchant Account   210

   Uploading APK file to Google Play   212

Distribution   214

   Through Other Markets   214

   Through Email   214

   Through Website link   214

Knowledge Check   216

Lab Exercise   217

Index   218

Preface

Welcome to *Android Development On Android Studio,* Al-Kathiri Khalid is a professional programming book writer, a software engineer and an international corporate trainer[1]. This book was an excitement to create as it reflects the changes to Android platform and provides recommended ways of learning, teaching and programming.

Features

This book is going to cover Android Studio Integrated Development Environment (IDE), Android SDK Tools, Android 6.0 Marshmallow Platform API Level 23 and above, Android 6.0 emulator system image, Google APIs, GitHub, Android Debug Bridge (ADB) commands, IntelliJ shortcut commands and Android Design patterns and Git version control system, which are all essential for an Android Developer Warrior.

This book is going to get you started into Android programming, from setting up your development environment, creating virtual devices, connecting actual / mobile devices and up to the stage of publishing your apps into play store.

Some of the chapters will start with a minimum of Android Jelly Bean instead of Android Lollipop depending on the highest current statistics collected from the Android Platform Versions Dashboard Pie Chart https://developer.android.com/about/dashboards/index.html, this is to ensure that your app will run on most devices connecting to Android Play Store.

---

[1] http://careers.stackoverflow.com/alkathirikhalid

About The Author

Al-Kathiri Khalid started learning computers at the age of 15 starting with MSDOS, he then enrolled at an Institute of Advanced Technology (IAT) and got certified as a PC technician with distinction grade, dealing with hardware allowed him to get his hands dirty which was productive and fun at the same time, hence this lead him to further his studies into B.Sc. (Hons.) in Electrical and Electronic Engineering where he was exposed to C++ programming. This Programming sparked and won his heart, this was something he could sit and create, behold it was MAGICAL!

The experience leads him to switch to B.Sc. (Hons.) in Computing where he was exposed to SDLC, UML, JAVA, JSP, SERVLETS, OOP, ORACLE 10g, MYSQL, DESIGN PATTERNS and a bunch of other things.

He volunteered to train his peers and orphanage for charity. He can still remember his supervisor encouraging him to take something totally new and challenging it felt more like "let's gamble on this kid's life" but it was a challenge he accepted so for his final year project he was assigned a task to learn Android on his own and build an Android *"Mobile Application for Users with Special Needs"*. This was with Android Eclair API 2.1. He is a strong supporter and user of Free and Open Source Systems (FOSS) which he uses to build web, mobile and desktop applications.

later in life He became one of the first in the world to be certified under the Google Web Academy program and train in South East Asia under My Uni Alliance Program. He has undertaken project after project both from work and freelance evolving corporate local & International training and programming. He has trained hundreds of candidates in Android programming clients such as HP, MRT, MIMOS, Prasarana etc.

Before You Begin

Ensure you have *JDK SE 7* (Java Development Kit Standard Edition) and above installed in your system. Java is an OS (Operating System) independent platform and a programming language, it runs on Windows, Mac OS X and Linux within a JVM (Java Virtual Machine).

Who Is This Book for?

This book is for *beginner, junior* and *advanced programmers* familiar with OOP (Object Oriented Programming) preferably in JAVA and client side programming in XML whom have no to little knowledge about Android and Android Studio. Knowledge on JAVA is essential in this book to understand concepts such as Object, Class, Inheritance, Interface, Package, Instantiation, Initialization, Variable, Operators, Control Flow Statements, Collections etc. while XML knowledge is also essential but not necessary.

How to Use This Book

This book will provide the necessary explanation on every even page number (2,4,6… etc.) and the necessary illustration, diagram or code on the following odd page number (3, 5, 7… etc.) for easy and optimum readability and ease of use to the reader, this book was written with the reader in mind.

JDK Installation

JDK 7 is required when developing for Android 5.0 and higher. To check if you have JDK installed and which version, open a terminal or command prompt and type javac -version Fig. 0.1.

If you get a message such as *'javac'* is not recognized as an internal or external command then you will need to go to the official site and grab the latest copy of JDK by downloading it from http://www.oracle.com/technetwork/java/javase/downloads/index.html Fig. 0.2.

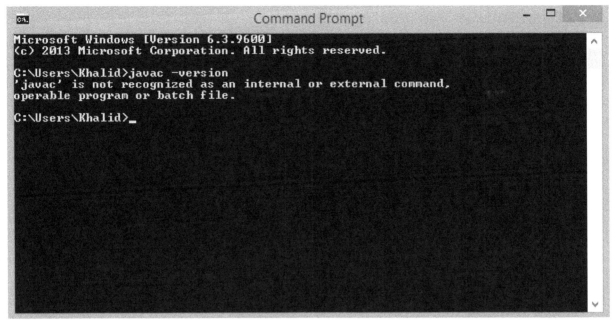

Fig. 0.1 | Checking Java Compiler Version.

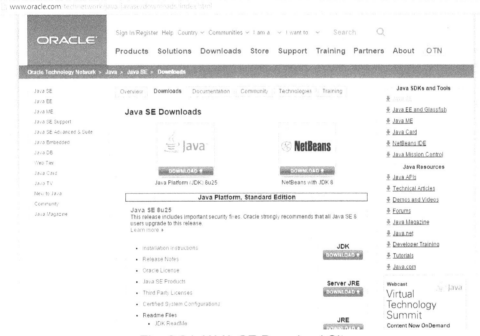

Fig. 0.2 | JAVA SE Download Site.

Java Path Setup

You may now run and install the JDK in your system and set *JAVA System Environment Path*, the instruction is provided in the official JAVASE Essential Tutorial on Path Setup https://docs.oracle.com/javase/tutorial/essential/environment/paths.html see also Fig. 0.3. for Windows. When you now run JAVASE commands such as javac -version from the command prompt your system will know where to look Fig. 0.4.

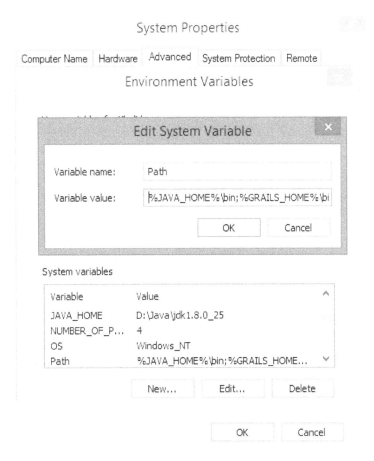

Fig. 0.3 | Java Path

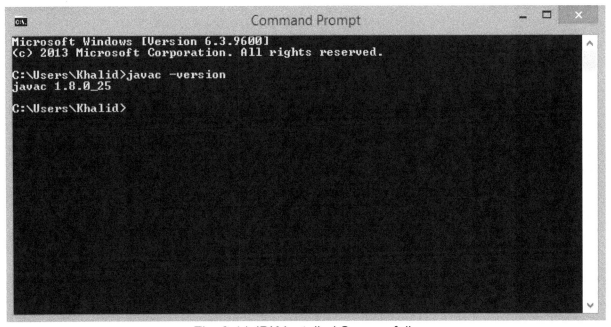

Fig. 0.4 | JDK Installed Successfully.

Chapter 1

Introduction

In this chapter we are going to cover the basic understanding of Android, Android Studio and what you will need to get started.

What is Android

Android is an open-source operating system based on Linux and used for smartphones, tablet computers, TV boxes and other devices. As the main hardware platform for Android is the ARMv7, ARMv8-A, x86 and MIPS architectures. Android 5.0 Lollipop, 64-bit variants of all platforms are supported in addition to the 32-bit variants. Since 2012, Android devices with Intel processors began to appear, including phones and tablets. At the same time gaining support for 64-bit platforms, Android was first made to run on 64-bit x86 and then on ARM64.

What is Android Studio

Android Studio is an integrated development environment (IDE) for the Android platform. It was first announced in May 2013 at the Google I/O conference by Ellie Powers who was the Google's Product Manager and later it was made as the official Android Development Environment on Dec 2014.

Android Studio was in early access preview stage starting from version 0.1 in May 2013, then entered beta stage starting from version 0.8 which was released in June 2014. The first stable build was released in December 2014, starting from version 1.0 based on JetBrains' IntelliJ IDEA software, the Android Studio is designed specifically for Android development only and It is available for download on Windows, Mac OS X and even Linux.

System Requirements

Windows	Mac OS X	Linux
<ul><li>Microsoft® Windows® 8/7/Vista/2003 (32 or 64-bit)</li><li>2 GB RAM minimum, 4 GB RAM recommended</li><li>400 MB hard disk space + at least 1 G for Android SDK, emulator system images, and caches</li><li>1280 x 800 minimum screen resolution</li><li>Java Development Kit (JDK) 7</li><li>Optional for accelerated emulator: Intel® processor with support for Intel® VT-x, Intel® EM64T (Intel® 64), and Execute Disable (XD) Bit functionality</li></ul>	<ul><li>Mac® OS X® 10.8.5 or higher, up to 10.9 (Mavericks)</li><li>2 GB RAM minimum, 4 GB RAM recommended</li><li>400 MB hard disk space</li><li>At least 1 GB for Android SDK, emulator system images, and caches</li><li>1280 x 800 minimum screen resolution</li><li>Java Runtime Environment 6</li><li>Java Development Kit (JDK) 7</li><li>Optional for accelerated emulator: Intel® processor with support for Intel® VT-x, Intel® EM64T (Intel® 64), and Execute Disable (XD) Bit functionality</li></ul>	<ul><li>GNOME or KDE desktop</li><li>GNU C Library (glibc) 2.11 or later</li><li>2 GB RAM minimum, 4 GB RAM recommended</li><li>400 MB hard disk space</li><li>At least 1 GB for Android SDK, emulator system images, and caches</li><li>1280 x 800 minimum screen resolution</li><li>Oracle® Java Development Kit (JDK) 7</li></ul>

Installation and Setup

There are a number of things you can install, update and customize for your Android development environment which will be influence by API requirements and developer taste.

The most crucial is Android Studio and Android SDK here we will cover one by one and provide good practical tips.

Installing Android Studio

Download Android Studio, go to the officail site https://developer.android.com/sdk/index.html or do a simple search *"Download Android Studio"* to get the latest version. Android Studio provides everything you need to start developing apps for Android, including the Android Studio IDE and the Android SDK tools.

Before you set up Android Studio, be sure you have installed JDK 6 or higher the JRE alone is not sufficient. JDK 7 is required when developing for Android 5.0 and JDK 8 is required for Android Studio 2.1. To check if you have JDK installed and which version it is, open a terminal and type javac -version. If the JDK is not available or the version is lower than Java 6 you will need to download it in order to develop Android Apps, see *Preface, JDK Installation* in this book.

Android Studio on Windows	Android Studio on Mac OSX	Android Studio on Linux
<ul><li>Launch the .exe file you just downloaded Fig. 1.1.</li><li>Follow the setup wizard to install Android Studio and any necessary SDK tools Fig .1.2.</li><li>On some Windows systems, the launcher script does not find where Java is installed. If you encounter this problem, you need to set an environment variable indicating the correct location, see Preface, Java Path Setup in this book.</li></ul>The individual tools and other SDK packages are saved outside the Android Studio application directory. If you need to access the tools directly, use a terminal to navigate to the location where they are installed. For example: \Users\<user>\AppData\Local\Android\sdk	<ul><li>Launch the .dmg file you just downloaded.</li><li>Drag and drop Android Studio into the Applications folder.</li><li>Open Android Studio and follow the setup wizard to install any necessary SDK tools.</li></ul>Depending on your security settings, when you attempt to open Android Studio, you might see a warning that says that the package is damaged and should be moved to the trash. If this happens, go to System Preferences > Security & Privacy and under Allow applications downloaded from, select Anywhere. Then open Android Studio again. If you need use the Android SDK tools from a command line, you can access them at: /Users/<user>/Library/Android/sdk/	<ul><li>Unpack the downloaded ZIP file into an appropriate location for your applications.</li><li>To launch Android Studio, navigate to the android-studio/bin/ directory in a terminal and execute studio.sh.</li><li>You may want to add android-studio/bin/ to your PATH environmental variable so that you can start Android Studio from any directory.</li><li>Follow the setup wizard to install any necessary SDK tools.</li></ul>

Fig. 1.1 | Android Studio Installation

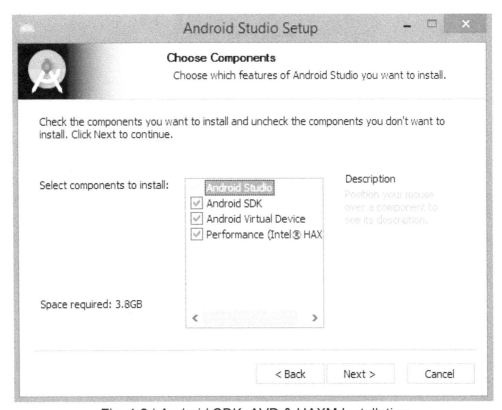

Fig. 1.2 | Android SDK, AVD & HAXM Installation

Follow the onscreen setup wizard by selecting the default values or do the necessary changes by modifying your Android Studio installation location and you may choose to import your settings from a previous version of Android Studio or have a clean installation Fig. 1.3. as you may see fit, once complete you may launch android studio Fig. 1.4.

Upon launching for the first time it is a good idea to check for latest updates if any by clicking on *Check for updates now* on the lower left corner Fig.1.4.

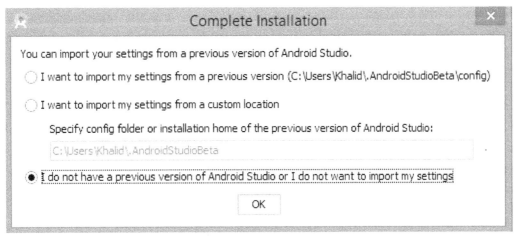

Fig. 1.3 | Clean Installation

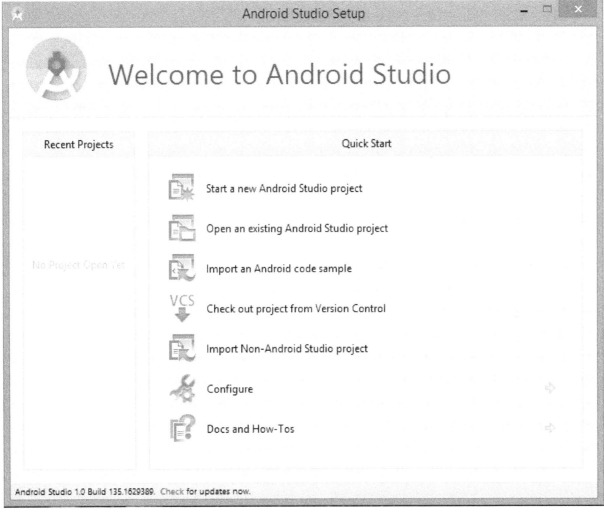

Fig. 1.4 | Launching Android Studio

Advance users may choose to specify the *Check for updates in channel* Stable, Beta, Dev or Canary, for long term development purposes Fig. 1.5. It is advisable to select Stable so that Android Studio IDE only updates once a stable patch is released this will avoid unforeseen bugs in the IDE which could temporarily slow your app development time.

In this book we are going to stick with the defaults values and leave the *Check for updates in channel* Beta option.

You may further go to Fig. 1.4. Configure > Settings and setup necessary environment for your development like *Version Control* such as GitHub, Git, CVS, Mercurial or Subversion Fig. 1.6. You may also explore other features such as *Appearance* and setup Android Studio to your liking.

Android Studio is now ready and loaded with the Android developer tools, but there are still a couple of packages you should add in order to make your Android System Development Kit complete by adding necessary packages which we are going to cover next.

TIP #1: Take note if you are involved in a long term project or working in a team, it is advisable to stick to updates in the *stable channel,* so as to avoid unforeseen disruptions due to regular updates that might interfere with your schedule development timing not only might you encounter a bug but also due to the fact that sometimes regular updates tend to be time consuming.

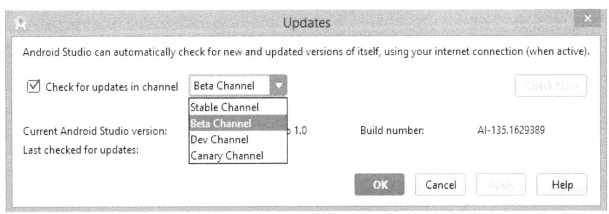

Fig. 1.5 | Android Studio Update Channels

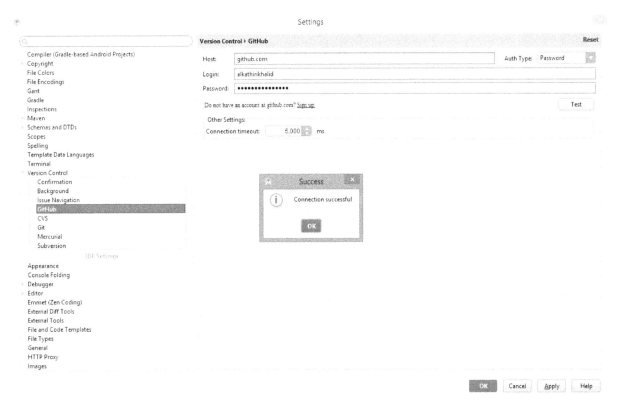

Fig.1.6 | Android Studio Settings

Adding SDK Packages

The SDK separates tools, platforms, and other components into packages you can download as needed using the Android SDK Manager. So before you can start, there are a few packages you should add to your Android Software Development Kit.

To start adding packages, launch the Android SDK Manager in one of the following ways:
- In Android Studio, click SDK Manager in the toolbar (Visible after you have start/open Android Studio Project).
- If you're not using Android Studio:
  - Windows: Double-click the SDK Manager.exe file at the root of the Android SDK directory \Users\<user>\AppData\Local\Android\sdk\SDK Manager.exe Fig. 1.7.
  - Mac/Linux: Open a terminal and navigate to the tools/ directory in the Android SDK, then execute android sdk.
- You could also do this in the terminal / command prompt to trigger an update by executing: tools\android.bat update sdk --no-ui Fig. 1.8. accept the license agreement and update will begin.

To install Platform-tools, Android platforms and other add-ons, you must have an Internet connection, so if you are planning to use the SDK while offline, do make sure to download the necessary components while online.

When you open the SDK Manager for the first time, several packages are selected by default. Leave these selected, there is no need to select all packages but only those which you require to develop your app:

Tools	Android <Version> <API>	Extra
<ul><li>Android SDK Tools</li><li>Android SDK Platform-tools</li><li>Android SDK Build-tools (highest version)</li></ul>	<ul><li>SDK Platform</li><li>Any System image for the emulator</li></ul>	<ul><li>Google Repository</li><li>Google Play services</li><li>Google USB Driver</li><li>Intel x86 Emulator Accelerator (HAXM Installer)</li></ul>

TIP #2: There is no harm in selecting all packages if your hardware can handle it, which will take around 50GB plus disk size and as more packages you have the more loading / startup time it will take to render your Android Studio apps UI view, which is based on the rendering SDK's you have installed, the message *"Initializing Rendering Library..."* will be visible on your app layout.

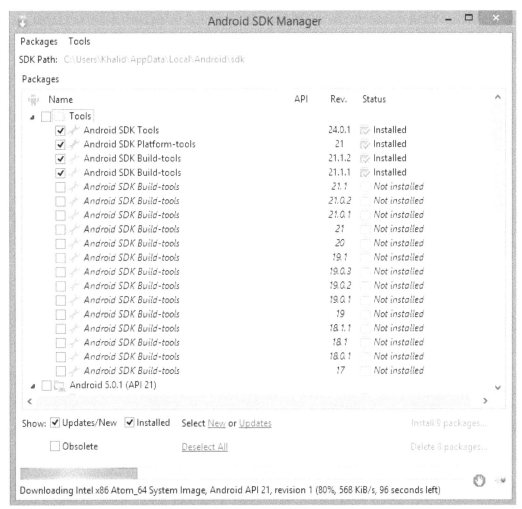

Fig. 1.7 | Adding SDK Packages

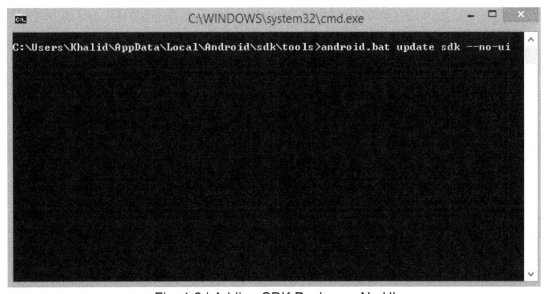

Fig. 1.8 | Adding SDK Packages No UI

Android SDK Path Setup

There are times you would want to update SDK or build your app from the terminal / command prompt without typing the full path, this will require you add the below to your system path Fig. 1.9:

- Users\<user>AppData\Local\Android\sdk\tools
- Users\<user>\AppData\Local\Android\sdk\platform-tools

Tools	Platform Tools
<ul><li>android</li><li>ddms</li><li>draw9patch</li><li>emulator</li><li>hierarchyviewer</li><li>jobb</li><li>lint</li><li>mksdcard</li><li>monitor</li><li>monkeyrunner</li><li>traceview</li><li>uiautomatorviewer</li></ul>	<ul><li>adb</li><li>dmtracedump</li><li>etc1tool</li><li>fastboot</li><li>hprof-conv</li><li>sqlite3</li></ul>

We will not cover all the tools and platform tools in this book, the ones we have covered is android for adding SDK Packages, others that we are going to cover later are ddms, adb, lint etc.

Once you have setup the Android SDK Path, you can confirm by typing path in your command prompt Fig. 1.10.

TIP #3: You may setup ANDROID_SDK_ROOT variable in your path and point it to the home directory of your android sdk folder such as "Users\<user>AppData\Local\Android\sdk" and then use %ANDROID_SDK_ROOT%\tools and %ANDROID_SDK_ROOT%\platform-tools as a shortcut in your path.

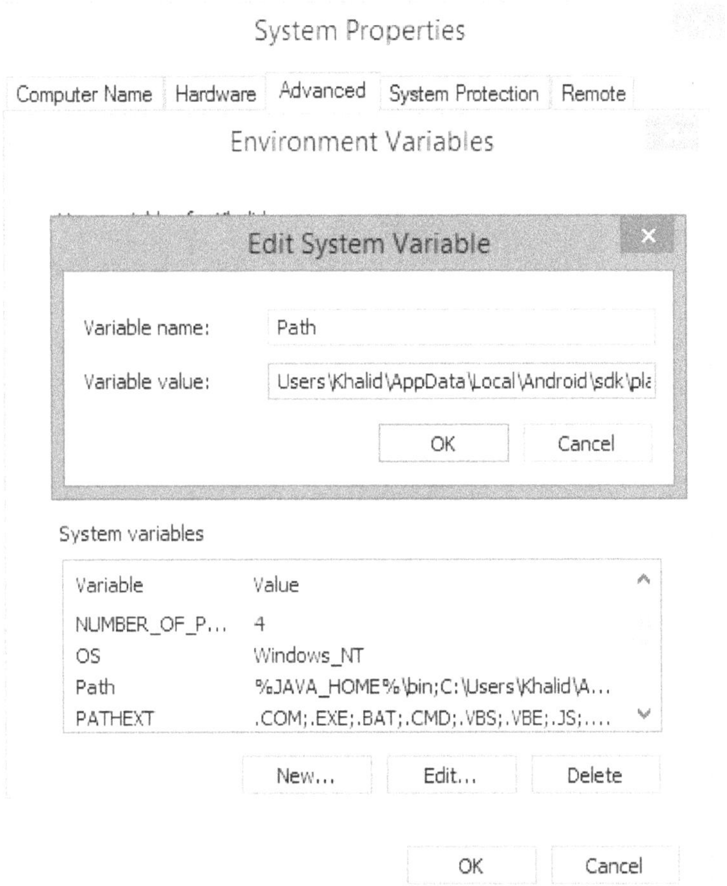

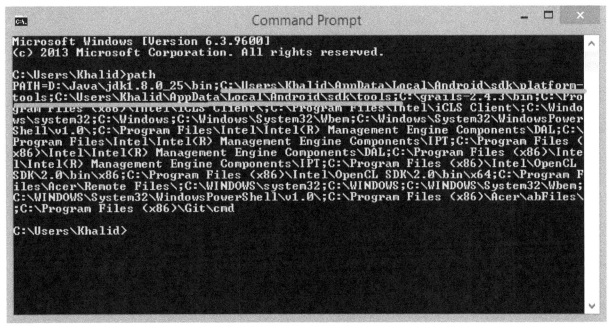

Fig. 1.9 | Android SDK Path Setup

Fig. 1.10 | Path Verification

Android Virtual Device

After Installation and setup, it is time to create Android Virtual Device (AVD) which is also referred as an Emulator to test run you Apps, you can access and run AVD Manager in a number of ways:

- Within your Android SDK, run SDK Manager
- Within Android Studio

  - Click AVD Manager icon in the toolbar, AVD Manager will popup Fig. 1.11.
  - or select Tools > Android > AVD Manager
- From command line, change directories to <sdk>/tools/ and execute: android avd or if you have followed the previous example on setting up your Android SDK Path Setup you won't have to change directory for any Android Commands Fig. 1.12.

The AVD Manager provides options on whether you want to create a virtual device based on the device definition of known devices such as Nexus 5, 6 etc. or you can create a custom device definition by providing your device configuration for your AVD.

You also have the option to create as many AVD's as you would like to use with the Android Emulator. In order to effectively test your apps, you should create an AVD that models each device type for which you have designed your app to support based on the App API. For example, you should create an AVD for each API level equal to and higher than the minimum version you have specified in your App manifest.

TIP #4: There is no difference in the virtual devices by launching AVD Manager either through Android Studio, command line or running AVD Manager directly in the SDK folder, even though they might appear different in the case of Fig. 1.11. and Fig. 1.12. The virtual devices themselves are being pulled and store in a central location Users\<user>\.android\avd they just have multiple ways of being accessed.

Fig. 1.11 | AVD Manager through Android Studio

Fig. 1.12 | AVD Manager through Command Line

Setup a Virtual Device

In this book we are going to cover AVD creation through the Android Studio IDE, to create an AVD is very straightforward, after you launch the AVD Manager Fig.1.11. follow the onscreen steps, to create an AVD based on the existing device definition to be specific Nexus 6.

- Click *Create Virtual Device* lower left on Fig. 1.11.
- A *Select Hardware* window will appear, select Nexus 6 as the Device Configuration Fig. 1.13. or any other you may see fit, and click Next.
- A *System Image* window will appear, select the desired system version for the AVD Fig. 1.14. this will set the API, ABI and Target. Click Next.
- Verify the configuration settings Fig. 1.15 and click Finish.

You could do other advance setting by clicking *Show Advanced Settings* and select a custom skin for the hardware profile or adjust another hardware settings Fig. 1.16.

TIP #5: If you are running your development environment on a PC and you have selected Intel as a System Image for your AVD, ensure you have installed sdk\extra\intel where you will find an Intel Emulator Accelerator / Hardware Accelerated Execution Manager (HAXM), run it and it will improve performance and speed on your development environment. Do select Google API System Image unlike Android alone this will have Google functionality i.e. location and map as you would on your Android Phone.

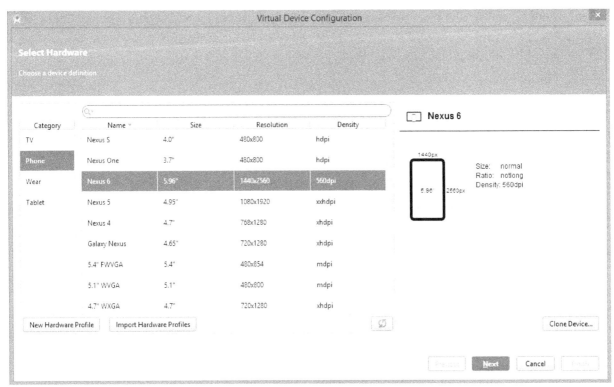

Fig. 1.13 | Hardware device configuration

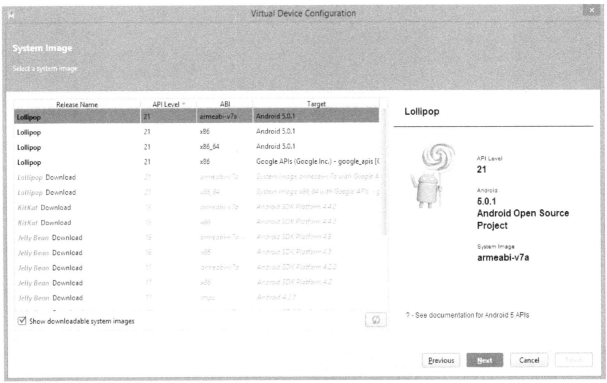

Fig 1.14. | System Image configuration

It is good practice to either enable *Use Host GPU* or *Store a snapshot for faster startup* Fig. 1.15. as it will improve AVD startup and loading time, depending on your environment hardware, ensure your system is above the minimum system requirement for Android apps development so as to see significant improvement on speed.

Enabling Use Host GPU will share your system graphics memory with Android which might have lagging effect on your system depending on the GPU you have in your development environment, so do make sure you have above minimum system requirement alternatively you could enable store a snapshot.

On PC, when you install and run Hardware Accelerated Execution Manager (HAXM) it will reserve a portion of your system memory for your AVD, ensure your development environment is above minimum system requirement so as to avoid starving your system of precious memory.

Alternatively, you could manually change the settings Fig. 1.16. to reduce your AVD Ram or other resource that you see fit but bear in mind that this will not reflect the physical Nexus 6 device you are trying to emulate and test run your app, finally it is always better to test run your app on an actual device if your run low on hardware resources or encounter performance issues.

AVD is handy when the device you are building an App on does not meet the latest API release, example such as the device you have is Android KitKat 4.4, and you want your app to also support Android Lollipop 5.0, it is recommended in order to know and test the look and feel on these latest release you can create and AVD.

To launch the AVD from the list in Android Virtual Device Manager, click the launch button ▷ in the far right of the AVD you just created under *Actions*, in this example Nexus 6.

TIP #6: If you plan to test run your app on AVD, ensure your launch your AVD first and let it run before you start on your app coding, as the initial launch consumes a significant amount of processing power (depending on your system and AVD setting) and time, it should be the first thing you launch and the last thing you close, speed has been improved with Android Studio 2.0 and Android Emulator 6.0.

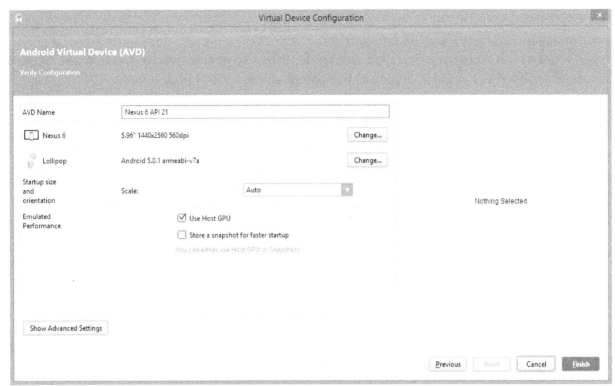

Fig. 1.15 | Verify Configuration

Fig. 1.16 | Advance Settings

Setup a Mobile Device

It is not necessary but highly recommend to test run your apps on a real device, as it will have its own processing power and memory and you would not need to share precious resources from your development environment which improves development efficiency and performance.

Real devices also have an advantage over AVD due to the fact that a real device might or might not have other peripherals such as front and back camera, accelerometer, pedometer and a bunch of other sensors depending on the device itself, whereas an AVD is limited in the sense that it might absolutely not have hardware for sensor hence external sensor peripherals will need to be installed along with its accompanied drivers.

To setup your device you must first:
- Enable *USB debugging* on your device.
  - On Devices running Android 3.2 or older, you can find the option under Settings > Applications > Development
  - On Devices running Android 4.0 and newer, you can find the option under Settings > Developer options
  - While on Devices running Android 4.2 and newer, Developer options is hidden by default and in order to make it available, go to Settings > About phone and tap *Build number* 7 times and Developer options will be visible in the previous screen, now go ahead and enable USB debugging Fig. 1.17.
- Plug in your device to your development machine with a USB cable. If you are developing on Windows, you might need to install the appropriate USB driver for your device. For further help on installing drivers for devices that are not detected, you will need to obtain the Original Equipment Manufacturers (OEM) USB Drivers.

In the event where your mobile device is one of the Android Developer Phones (ADP) such as a Nexus One, or a Nexus S, then you will need the Google USB Driver Fig. 1.18.

When you connect a device running Android 4.2.2 or higher for the first time to your computer, the device shows a dialog asking whether to accept an RSA key that will allow debugging through your computer. This security mechanism ensures that debugging and adb commands cannot be executed unless you unlock your device and accept the RSA for debugging on that particular machine. This feature is included in adb version 1.0.31 and above.

If you are developing on Windows using a devices other than the ADP, you can obtain a list of Original Equipment Manufacturers (OEM) that Android has provided on the Android Developer site: http://developer.android.com/tools/extras/oem-usb.html#Drivers.

TIP #7: Take note that the list is not exhaustive, if you cannot find a support link for your device, you will need to go to your device site and obtain instructions and further support.

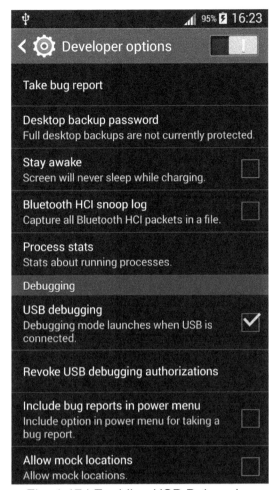

Fig. 1.17 | Enabling USB Debugging

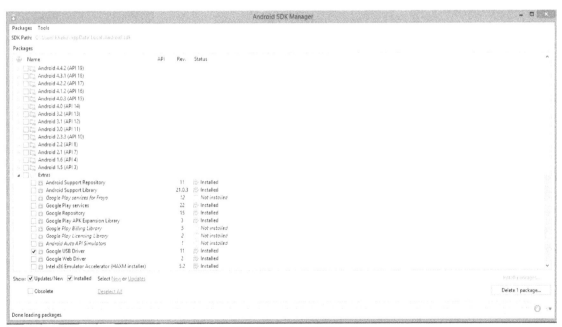

Fig. 1.18 | Google USB Driver

Quick Commands

After you have covered the previous topics on Installation and Setup, you are ready to beginning Android Application Development, this topic is not necessary but highly recommended for those who are new to IntelliJ IDEA and Android SDK (Quick Commands / Shortcut Keys / Prompt / Terminal Commands), grasping them will allow you to code faster and efficient while developing your apps.

Android Studio Keyboard Shortcuts

The most common tasks would be to complete code or a statement, insert a new file or override a method, generate a getter and setter method, finding a Class or a file, code duplication etc.

Keyboard Shortcuts	Description
Ctrl + Space	Code completion
Ctrl + Shift + Space	Smart Code completion
Ctrl + Shift + Enter	Smart Statement completion
Alt + Insert	Multiple use depending where you perform: Insert a new file, Override Method, Generate code such as Getters, Setters, Constructors, hashCode/equals, toString
Ctrl + N	Find a Class or File by name
Ctrl + D	Duplicate the current line or selection
Alt + Enter	Quick fixes such as imports
Ctrl + Alt + L	Reformat code
Ctrl + Q	Lookup documentation

The above keyboard shortcuts should get you started.

TIP #8: You can make it a habit to learn and apply at least 2-3 keymap at a time, do not over emphasize the need to learn them all at once, learning and applying the keymap as you progress will allow you to develop muscle memory that will last a long time and you will be able to instinctively use them as you progress.

Android Tools and Commands

Android has a variety of tools that can be used, these tools are all categorized either under SDK Tools or Platform Tools, see *Android SDK Path Setup* in this book. SDK tools are platform independent and they are required no matter which Android platform you are developing on while Platform tools are customized to support the features of the latest Android platform, most of these tools are visually accessible through the Android Studio IDE.

You can also build and run Android apps through the command line, here we are going to briefly cover some of the common commands that are helpful to most developers.

Android

- Create, delete and view Android Virtual Devices
- Create and update Android projects
- Update your Android SDK with new platforms, add-ons, and documentation

Syntax:

        android [global options] action [action options]

Options:

        -s Silent mode: only errors are printed out
        -h Usage help
        -v Verbose mode: errors, warnings and informational messages are printed

Command	Description
android avd	Launch AVD Manager
android sdk	Launch SDK Manager
android update adb	Updates Android Debug Bridge to support the USB devices declared in the SDK add-ons (you will need to kill ADB server and restart it)
android update sdk	Updates the SDK by suggesting new platforms to install if available

ADB

- Allows you to communicate with Virtual Device or connected Android Device. It is a client server program that has three components:
  - A client: this runs on your development machine. You can invoke a client from a shell by issuing an adb command.
  - A server: this runs as a background process on your development machine. And manages communication between the client and the adb daemon running on a virtual or actual device.
  - A daemon: this runs as a background process on each virtual or actual device instance.

Syntax:

adb [-d|-e|-s <serialNumber>] <command>

Options:

-d Direct an adb command to the only attached USB device

-e Direct an adb command to the only running emulator instance

-s Direct an adb command to a specific emulator/device instance, by its assigned serial number example emulator-5554 or emulator-5556 e.t.c.

Command	Description
adb devices	Shows a list of all attached virtual or actual device instances
adb version	Shows the adb version number
adb help	Shows a list of supported adb commands
adb start-server	Starts adb server process
adb kill-server	Terminates adb server process
adb shell	Starts shell in the remote target virtual or actual device instance

If there is only one virtual device running or only one actual device connected, the adb command is sent to it by default. In the event you have multiple virtual devices running and or multiple actual devices attached, you need to use the -d, -e, or -s option to specify the target device.

Lint

- This is a static code analysis tool that looks through your Android project source files for potential bugs, optimization, improvements for correctness, security, performance, usability, accessibility, and localization such as if you included translation to support other languages.

Syntax:

lint [flags] <project directory>

Options:

--disable <list> Disable checking for a specific list of issues.

--enable <list> Check for all the default issues supported by lint

--check <list> Check for a specific list of issues, list must be comma separated

--html <filename> Generate an HTML report.

--xml <filename> Generate an XML report

--show List the ID and verbose description for issues that can be checked by lint

--version Show lint version

Commands	Description
lint myproject	Scan all Java and XML files in my project directory and its subdirectories, show result in console
lint myproject --html <filename>	Scan all Java and XML files in my project directory and its subdirectories, show result in html <filename>

You can apply the following annotation to the source files of your project:
- Disable lint checking for a specific Java class or method, just use the @SuppressLint annotation
- Disable lint checking for specific sections of your XML file, just use the tools:ignore attribute

Other powerful and recommended tools apart from lint are proguard which shrinks, optimizes, and obfuscates your code for more security and prevents reverse engineering your code by removing unused code and renaming classes, fields, and methods with semantically obscure names. Another one monkeyrunner which test apps and devices at the functional level.

With these simple but yet powerful productive shortcuts and commands you are on your way to be an effective and efficient Android App developer, by knowing your Android Development tools or any other development tools you are working with, gives you a head start over other new developers.

Knowledge Check

1. What is the advantage of using an IDE like Android Studio?
2. How would you troubleshoot an Android phone that is not detected by ADB?
3. When would it be suitable to use AVD over an Actual Device?
4. Explain the difference between a Simulator and an Emulator?
5. Is Android AVD a Simulator or an Emulator based on your findings?
6. You found a developer pressing Alt+Enter in Android Studio, what do you think he was trying to achieve? Is there a better way?
7. Explain what does pressing Ctrl+Alt+L do while programming in Android Studio?
8. What is the first thing you need to do to an Android mobile device before you start testing an app?
9. When testing your app on AVD what is the recommended Android OS running on the AVD?
10. Explain what is available in Android SDK directories

Lab Exercise

1. Install Android Studio
2. Update SDK using SDK Manager
3. Ensure you have selected Tool, Extra, Android target SDK (Your Application Target i.e. 16) and Current Android SDK (Latest Android OS)
4. Create an AVD using latest Android release
5. Setup an Android Mobile device if you have one

Remember you do not have to download everything in the SDK Manager, only the tools that you need as explained in this book.

Chapter 2

Introduction

In this chapter we are going to look on how to develop Android Applications in Android Studio, see the basic structure, introduce you to your first skeletal application, generated files, code, available layout and launch your first app on your virtual or actual device.

Platform Version and Distribution

This provides information on the relative number of devices that share some characteristic, like version or screen size. The data is helpful for developers and marketing personnel to prioritize efforts for in order to support different devices at the same time knowing which devices are actually connecting and active in Google Play. Fig. 2.1.

As seen in the pie chart jelly Bean still has a huge portion to be considered as the minimum SDK for an App without sacrificing too much on API, whereby Froyo will allow you to cover almost 99.9% to all the devices connection to Google Play ecosystem. Fig. 2.2.

Version	Codename	API	Distribution
2.2	Froyo	8	0.1%
2.3.3 - 2.3.7	Gingerbread	10	1.5%
4.0.3 - 4.0.4	Ice Cream Sandwich	15	1.4%
4.1.x	Jelly Bean	16	5.6%
4.2.x		17	7.7%
4.3		18	2.3%
4.4	KitKat	19	27.7%
5.0	Lollipop	21	13.1%
5.1		22	21.9%
6.0	Marshmallow	23	18.7%

Fig. 2.1 | Distribution Table

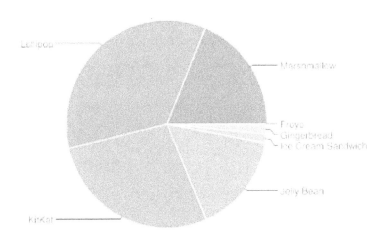

Fig. 2.2 | Distribution Pie Chart
As of September 5, 2016.
Any versions with less than 0.1% distribution are not shown.

How to Start Android App Development

Immediately after setting up your development Environment you are ready to start developing Android apps there are a few ways to achieve this but one has more advantage over the other and is mostly prefer.

Through Android Studio IDE

Start Android Studio and select *Start a new Android Studio project* as seen previously in Fig. 1.4.

In the *Configure your new project* screen Fig. 2.3. You will need to provide:
- Application Name: This is the app name that appears to users on Play Store and Device
- Company Domain: This is your domain name it acts as a unique qualifier that will be used as the package name for each new project you create
- Package Name: This is the fully qualified name for your project it is the same rules as those for naming packages in the Java, this must be unique across all packages installed on the Android
- Project Location: This is the directory on your computer that the project files reside

In the *Select the form factors your app will run on* screen Fig. 2.4. You will need to select:
- The box for Phone and Tablet, as we will be building a phone/tablet App
- Select API 16: Android 4.1 (Jelly Bean) as the Minimum SDK. This will be our earliest version of Android that this app supports

TIP #9: To support as many devices as possible, you should regularly check Android Dashboard see *Features in Preface and Platform version and distribution,* all the data presented on the Pie Chart are showing devices connecting to Android Play Store so do set this to the lowest version available that allows your app to provide its core features any lower than that would be sacrificing on API but we want to also reach as many devices as possible, every new Android release has new API features.

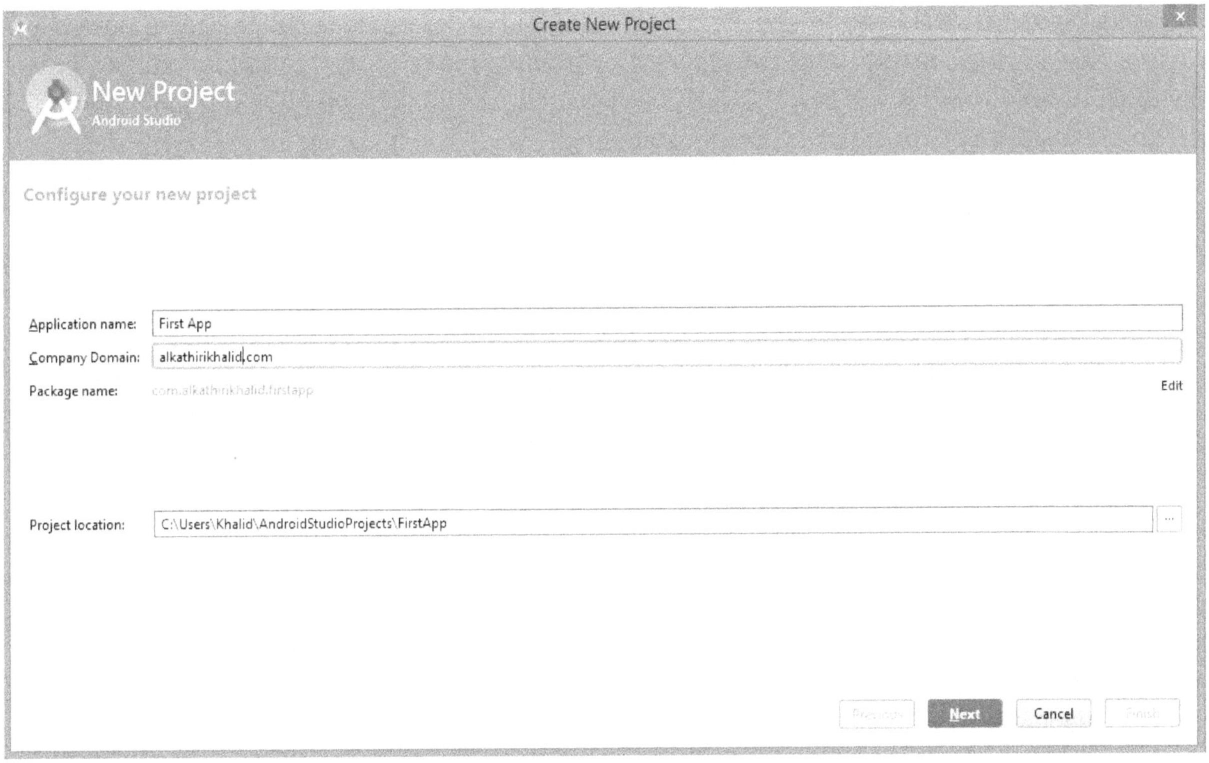

Fig. 2.3 | Configure your new project

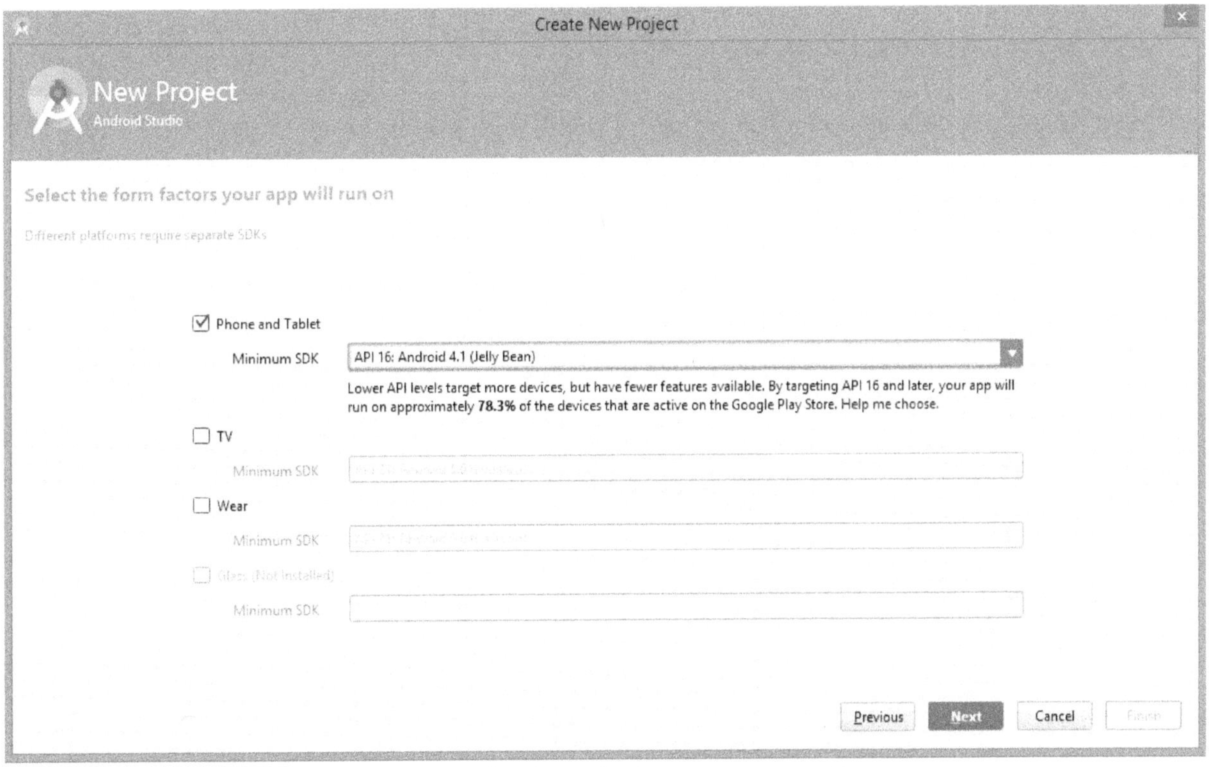

Fig. 2.4 | Select the form factors your app will run on

After clicking Next, you will need to specify an activity for your application, an activity is basically what your users see on their screen and can interact with your app. For this example, we will have one activity *Main Activity* which is the entry point to our app, just like in Java we have the main method, later we will go into details about an activity and its states.

Android studio provides multiple templates for an app activity and generates the code for your app, the activity presented are the most commonly applied in most apps, so choose one that you need for your app.

For this *skeleton first app* we will stick to *Blank Activity*, depending on the activity you choose the enormous generated code can be overwhelming and confusing for most beginners' level Android Developers.

In the *Add an activity to mobile* Screen Fig. 2.5. You will need to select:
- *Blank Activity*, and click Next.

In the *Choose options for your new file* Screen Fig. 2.6. You will need to provide:
- Activity Name: This is a java file referred as an Activity class which starts the activity and loads your layout file
- Layout Name: This is a XML layout file for the activity you added when you created the project, users will see this layout on screen with other views if available on your layout
- Title: This is a string of words users will see on the layout you created
- Menu Resource Name: This is also an XML file which will hold your menu bar items

Leave these values to default and *Click Finish*. To put it in simple terms, basically a static xml file named *activity_main.xml* (View) is backed by a dynamic java file/class named *MainActivity.java* (Controller) by doing this, it gives access and control to developers to manipulate objects/views on the layout hence the screen without dumping all code into one place, this in turn gives a sense of screen responsiveness to users Fig. 2.7 (Without model / Data source). Android was built with MVC model in mind but it's up to the developer to enforce it.

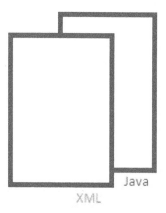

Fig. 2.7 | Android dynamic nature

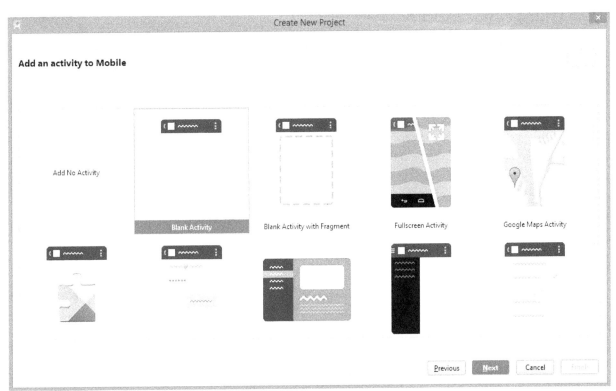

Fig. 2.5 | Add a Blank Activity

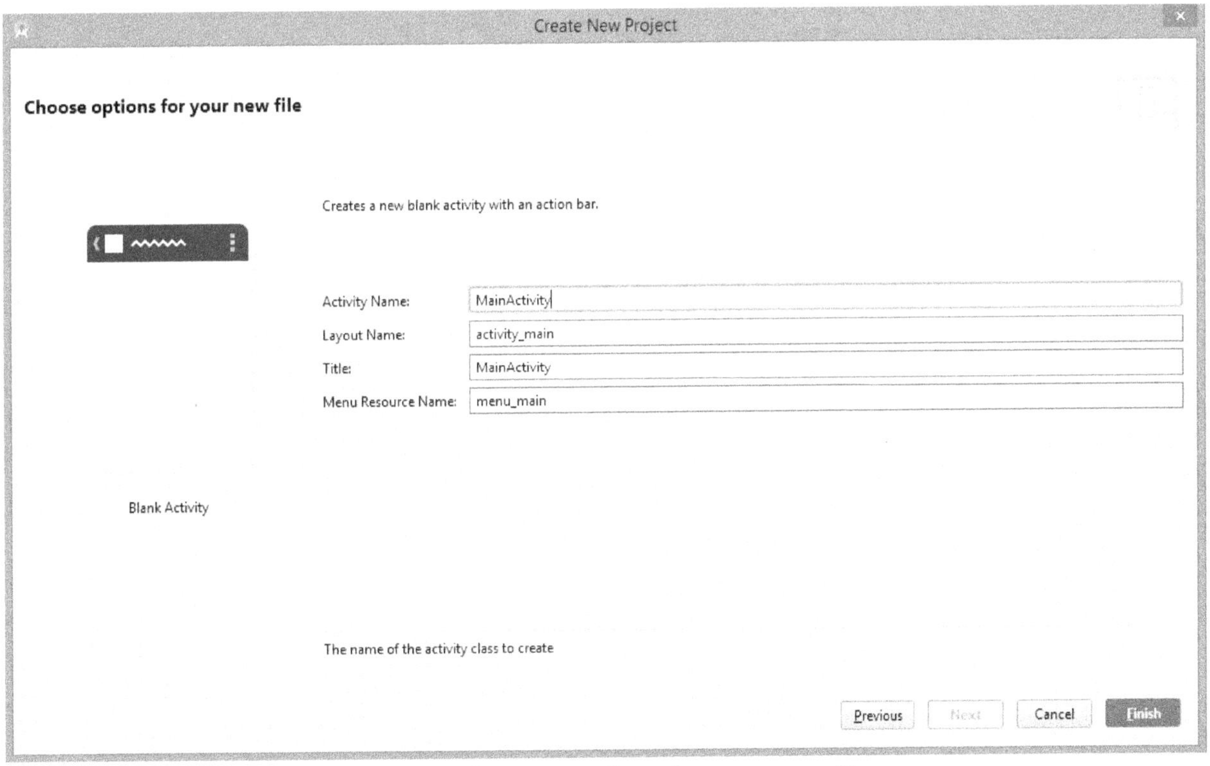

Fig. 2.6 | Choose options for your new file

Android will generate your app structure and files, and present them on Android Studio for the initial loading, take note the initial loading will take time as elaborate on TIP #2, after the build is completed you will have your first Android "Hello World", app based on our skeleton first app Fig. 2.8.

Through Command Line

You could alternatively create an app through command line by using android in Android SDK Tools, since we already covered on *Android SDK Path Setup* in Chapter 1, we can easily go ahead and use android command without changing directory.

First we will need to see the available Android Platform that have been downloaded for the SDK see *Adding SDK Packages* in Chapter 1, you will need this to specify the Android target.

Execute Fig. 2.8.: android list targets

TIP #10: You use the highest version possible. Since setting the build target to the latest version allows you to optimize your app for the latest devices.

Execute Fig. 2.9.: android create project --target android-21 --name FirstApp --path D:/MyFirstApp --activity MainActivity --package com.alkathirikhalid.firstapp

Do compare both applications, the one that you create *Through Android Studio IDE* and the one *Through Command Line*, you will notice the latter is missing some files that is because Android Studio uses a build system based on Gradle that provides flexibility, customized build variants, dependency resolution, and much more. This means that the app we create through command line basically are generated files and not an actual build app hence it cannot be pushed to our devices yet, later on we will need to tackle this, see *Launch Android App Through Command Line*.

TIP #11: These commands are compatible regardless of what operating system you are developing on, android command will execute on Mac, PC and Linux.

```
Microsoft Windows [Version 6.3.9600]
(c) 2013 Microsoft Corporation. All rights reserved.

C:\Users\Khalid>android list targets
Available Android targets:
----------
id: 1 or "android-18"
     Name: Android 4.3.1
     Type: Platform
     API level: 18
     Revision: 3
     Skins: HVGA, QVGA, WQVGA400, WQVGA432, WSVGA, WVGA800 (default), WVGA854, W
XGA720, WXGA800, WXGA800-7in
 Tag/ABIs : default/armeabi-v7a
----------
id: 2 or "android-19"
     Name: Android 4.4.2
     Type: Platform
     API level: 19
     Revision: 4
     Skins: HVGA, QVGA, WQVGA400, WQVGA432, WSVGA, WVGA800 (default), WVGA854, W
XGA720, WXGA800, WXGA800-7in
 Tag/ABIs : default/armeabi-v7a, default/x86
----------
id: 3 or "android-20"
     Name: Android 4.4W.2
     Type: Platform
     API level: 20
     Revision: 2
     Skins: HVGA, QVGA, WQVGA400, WQVGA432, WSVGA, WVGA800 (default), WVGA854, W
XGA720, WXGA800, WXGA800-7in, AndroidWearRound, AndroidWearSquare
 Tag/ABIs : android-wear/x86
----------
id: 4 or "android-21"
     Name: Android 5.0.1
     Type: Platform
     API level: 21
     Revision: 2
     Skins: HVGA, QVGA, WQVGA400, WQVGA432, WSVGA, WVGA800 (default), WVGA854, W
XGA720, WXGA800, WXGA800-7in, AndroidWearRound, AndroidWearSquare, AndroidWearRo
und, AndroidWearSquare
 Tag/ABIs : android-tv/armeabi-v7a, android-wear/armeabi-v7a, android-wear/x86,
default/armeabi-v7a, default/x86, default/x86_64
----------
```

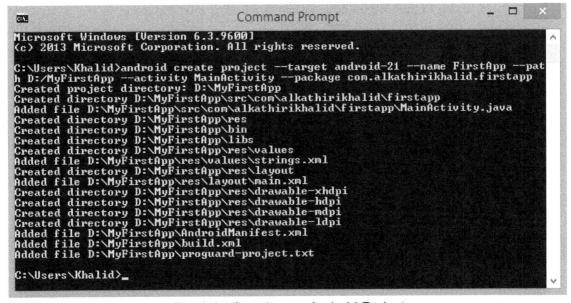

Fig. 2.8 | Listing available Android Targets

```
Microsoft Windows [Version 6.3.9600]
(c) 2013 Microsoft Corporation. All rights reserved.

C:\Users\Khalid>android create project --target android-21 --name FirstApp --pat
h D:/MyFirstApp --activity MainActivity --package com.alkathirikhalid.firstapp
Created project directory: D:\MyFirstApp
Created directory D:\MyFirstApp\src\com\alkathirikhalid\firstapp
Added file D:\MyFirstApp\src\com\alkathirikhalid\firstapp\MainActivity.java
Created directory D:\MyFirstApp\res
Created directory D:\MyFirstApp\bin
Created directory D:\MyFirstApp\libs
Created directory D:\MyFirstApp\res\values
Added file D:\MyFirstApp\res\values\strings.xml
Created directory D:\MyFirstApp\res\layout
Added file D:\MyFirstApp\res\layout\main.xml
Created directory D:\MyFirstApp\res\drawable-xhdpi
Created directory D:\MyFirstApp\res\drawable-hdpi
Created directory D:\MyFirstApp\res\drawable-mdpi
Created directory D:\MyFirstApp\res\drawable-ldpi
Added file D:\MyFirstApp\AndroidManifest.xml
Added file D:\MyFirstApp\build.xml
Added file D:\MyFirstApp\proguard-project.txt

C:\Users\Khalid>_
```

Fig. 2.9 | Creating an Android Project

How to Launch Android App

After creating your Android App either through the Android Studio IDE or through the Command line, it is time to test run your skeleton first app on either a virtual device or a real device. As explained in *Setup a Virtual Device* and *Setup a Mobile Device* Chapter 1, you may start your AVD or connect your mobile device or both.

Launch Android App Through Android Studio IDE

- Select your project file <app> and click Run ▶ from the toolbar Fig. 2.10.
- In the Choose Device screen that appears Fig. 2.11. Select the *Choose a running device* for a Mobile Device or *Launch emulator* radio button for Virtual Device, and click OK.

Android Studio installs the app on your chosen device and starts it.

Launch Android App Through Command Line

Change directories to the root of your Android project and execute:
- **On Windows:** gradlew assembleDebug
- **On Mac and Linux:** chmod +x gradlew **and** ./gradlew assembleDebug

Then execute:
- **On Windows, Mac or Linux:** adb install bin/FirstApp-debug.apk

After that open your device, locate FirstApp and open it. The full path for bin/FirstApp-debug.apk is FirstApp\app\build\outputs\apk\app-debug.apk Fig. 2.12. All new Android projects will include gradlew *gradle wrapper* script in the root directory of your Android project folder, without this you will not be able to do both of the above.

There are two modes of signing an app in android using either:
- assembleDebug this is for testing and debugging purposes, you can build in debug mode and immediately install it on a device for testing. Here the build tools automatically sign your application with a debug key and optimize the package with zipalign
- assembleRelease this is to release and distribute your application to users or distribution platforms such as Play Store.

For testing and development purposes we will be covering on debugging mode until such time when we release our application on Play Store, Android uniquely generates the debug key for every machine and it can be located at Users\<user>\.android\debug.keystore while release key will be manually generated by the developer.

TIP #12: In the event where you have both emulator running and a mobile device connected you can use -s or -d option respectively see ADB, in Chapter 1.

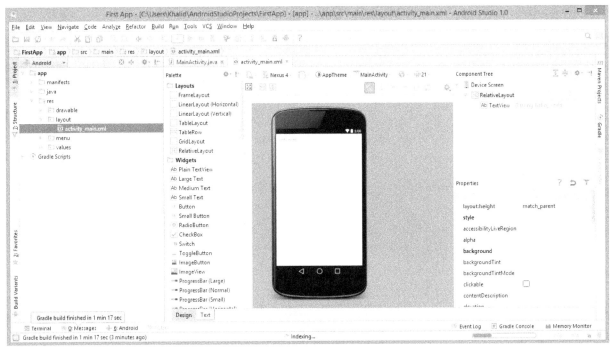

Fig. 2.10 | FirstApp Project

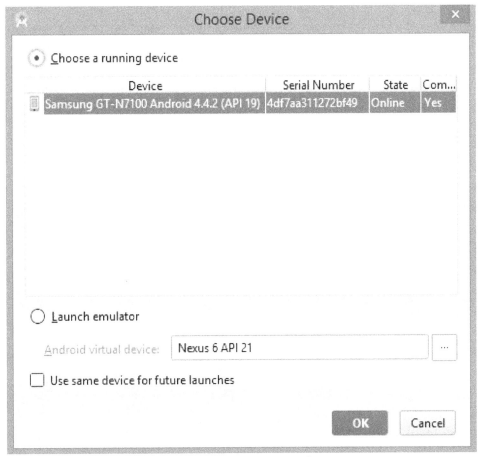

Fig. 2.11 | Choose Device Screen

Understanding Android App Structure

Android project is structured into folders Fig. 2.13. Here we are going to look at the folders and files that resides in it. For the purpose of introduction, the folders that we are keen to interact with through Android Studio IDE will be presented here.

Folders

- app ~ /java: This is where MainActivity.java and other Java classes reside
- app ~/res: This is where resources resides such as layouts, drawable/icons, menus, values etc.

Files

As depicted in Fig. 2.14.:

- app/src/main/res/layout/activity_main.xml: This is the XML layout file for the activity you added when you created the project
- app/src/main/java/com.alkathirikhalid.firstapp/MainActivity.java: This is the java file which starts the activity and loads the layout file
- app/src/res/AndroidManifest.xml: This is the file that describes the fundamental characteristics of the app and defines each of its components
- app/build.gradle: There is a build.gradle file for each module of your project, as well as a build.gradle file for the entire project. we are interested in the build.gradle file for the module, in this case the app module. This is where your app build dependencies are specified
- drawable-hdpi/: Directory for drawable objects images such as bitmaps that are designed for high-density
- layout/: Directory for files that define your app user interface layout such as activity_main.xml, which describes a basic layout for the MyActivity class
- values/: Directory for other XML files that contain a collection of resources, such as string, style and even dimension

Fig. 2.14 | Android Folders and Files

Fig. 2.12 | Launch Android App Through Command Line

Analyzing App Source Code

Based on FirstApp source code, by now you have your skeletal first application running on your AVD or physical devices, let us now analyze by using inline comments and better understand the generated code, we are going to concentrate on these files for now:

- MainActivity.java
- activity_main.xml
- AndroidManifest.xml
- Build.gradle (Module: app)

Main Activity Class

Based on MainActivity.java source code.

```java
package com.alkathirikhalid.firstapp;

import android.support.v7.app.ActionBarActivity;
import android.os.Bundle;
import android.view.Menu;
import android.view.MenuItem;

public class MainActivity extends ActionBarActivity {
    @Override
    protected void onCreate(Bundle savedInstanceState) {
        super.onCreate(savedInstanceState);
        // The code below sets our content to our layout xml file
        setContentView(R.layout.activity_main);
    }
    @Override
    public boolean onCreateOptionsMenu(Menu menu) {
        // Inflate the menu; this adds items to the action bar if it is present
        getMenuInflater().inflate(R.menu.menu_main, menu);
        return true;
    }
    @Override
    public boolean onOptionsItemSelected(MenuItem item) {
        // The action bar will automatically handle clicks on the Home/Up button, so long
        // as you specify a parent activity in AndroidManifest.xml
        int id = item.getItemId();
        // noinspection SimplifiableIfStatement
        if (id == R.id.action_settings) {
            return true;
        }
        return super.onOptionsItemSelected(item);
    }
}
```

Fig. 2.13 | Android Project Structure

The bare minimum code for our application to function is basically onCreate() method, the MainActivity.java code can be edited and do the one thing that we need it to do for now and that is to set our content to our layout xml file.

```java
package com.alkathirikhalid.firstapp;

import android.support.v7.app.ActionBarActivity;
import android.os.Bundle;

public class MainActivity extends ActionBarActivity {

    @Override
    protected void onCreate(Bundle savedInstanceState) {
        super.onCreate(savedInstanceState);
        // The code below sets our content to our layout xml file
        setContentView(R.layout.activity_main);
    }
}
```

TIP #13: When you build your application, your MainActivity will be set to extend either one of these class: Activity, AppCompactActivity or ActionBarActivity (deprecated). For new devices Activity will work fine but for other devices running older versions of Android your app won't appear as expected, Android has developed a set of support version to allow new features to not only work on new Android devices but also devices that runs previous version of Android from Android API level 7.

Example: android.support.v7.app.AppCompatActivity

Further information can be accessed from Android Support Library links:
- https://developer.android.com/tools/support-library/setup.html
- https://developer.android.com/tools/support-library/features.html

Activity Layout

Based on activity_main.xml layout file, here we have two objects, one is a ViewGroup and the other is a View, a ViewGroup is a holder that holds together and organize in an orderly fashion: either other ViewGroup's or View's, while a View is an actual representation of an object Fig. 2.15.

The two objects are RelativeLayout (ViewGroup) and a TextView (View), let us analyse some of the common important attributes and constants for these ViewGroup's and View's.

```xml
<RelativeLayout xmlns:android="http://schemas.android.com/apk/res/android"
    xmlns:tools="http://schemas.android.com/tools"
    android:layout_width="match_parent"
    android:layout_height="match_parent"
    android:paddingBottom="@dimen/activity_vertical_margin"
    android:paddingLeft="@dimen/activity_horizontal_margin"
    android:paddingRight="@dimen/activity_horizontal_margin"
    android:paddingTop="@dimen/activity_vertical_margin"
    tools:context=".MainActivity">

    <TextView
        android:layout_width="wrap_content"
        android:layout_height="wrap_content"
        android:text="@string/hello_world" />

</RelativeLayout>
```

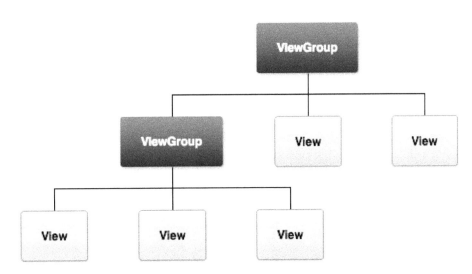

Fig. 2.15 | ViewGroup and View Objects

Attribute	Description
android:layout_width	Specifies the width of the ViewGroup or View
android:layout_height	Specifies the height of the ViewGroup or View
android:padding	Sets the padding, in pixels, of all four edges, this may also be a reference to a resource or theme attribute
tools:context	This attribute is typically set on the root element in a layout XML file, and records which activity the layout is associated with at design time, since obviously a layout can be used by more than one layout. This will for example be used by the layout editor to guess a default theme, since themes are defined in the Manifest and are associated with activities, not layouts. You can use the same dot prefix as in manifests to just specify the activity class without the full application package name as a prefix substitute context with: listitem / listheader / listfooter, ignore, targetApi, locale, layout, showIn, menu, actionBarNavMode
android:text	Text of string representing a title, this may also be a reference to a resource

The Attribute layout_width and layout_height have only three constant values that can be used for either the ViewGroup or View.

Constant	Description
fill_parent	This constant is deprecated starting from API Level 8 and is replaced by match_parent, the view should be as big as its parent minus padding
match_parent	Introduced in API Level 8, the view should be as big as its parent minus padding
wrap_content	The view should be only big enough to enclose its content plus padding

Android Manifest File

Based on AndroidManifest.xml file, the Manifest file is one of the most important file that Android system looks for in order to get information on how to set, launch and navigate through the application.

- It declares the permissions that others are required to have in order to interact with the applications components
- It declares the minimum level of the Android API that the application requires
- It lists the libraries that the application must be linked against
- It names the Java package / unique identifier for the application
- It describes the components of the application: such as activities, services, broadcast receivers, and content providers
- It determines which processes will host application components
- It declares which permissions the application must have in order to access protected parts of the API and interact with other applications

```xml
<?xml version="1.0" encoding="utf-8"?>
<manifest xmlns:android="http://schemas.android.com/apk/res/android"
    package="com.alkathirikhalid.firstapp">
    <!--Application Level defined as backup true, launcher icon, the app label and it's theme-->
    <application
        android:allowBackup="true"
        android:icon="@drawable/ic_launcher"
        android:label="@string/app_name"
        android:theme="@style/AppTheme">
        <!--Activity Level we only have one Activity and that is MainActivity, the action specifies
this is the entry point into our app and Category  specifies this will be the Launcher Activity
when user clicks on the icon in their device-->
        <activity
            android:name=".MainActivity"
            android:label="@string/app_name">
            <intent-filter>
                <action android:name="android.intent.action.MAIN" />

                <category android:name="android.intent.category.LAUNCHER" />
            </intent-filter>
        </activity>
        <!--Activity Level End-->
    </application>
    <!--Application Level End-->
</manifest>
```

A manifest file can have other elements, below is a list of all the Android manifest elements:

<action>
<activity>
<activity-alias>
<application>
<category>
<data>
<grant-uri-permission>
<instrumentation>
<intent-filter>
<manifest>
<meta-data>
<permission>
<permission-group>
<permission-tree>
<provider>
<receiver>
<service>
<supports-screens>
<uses-configuration>
<uses-feature>
<uses-library>
<uses-permission>
<uses-sdk>

TIP #14: All the elements that can be in the manifest file are fixed, as listed above and you cannot add any other elements or attributes to the manifest.

Manifest File Structure

```xml
<?xml version="1.0" encoding="utf-8"?>

<manifest>

   <uses-permission />
   <permission />
   <permission-tree />
   <permission-group />
   <instrumentation />
   <uses-sdk />
   <uses-configuration />
   <uses-feature />
   <supports-screens />
   <compatible-screens />
   <supports-gl-texture />

   <application>
      <activity>
         <intent-filter>
            <action />
            <category />
            <data />
         </intent-filter>
         <meta-data />
      </activity>
      <activity-alias>
         <intent-filter> Something goes here </intent-filter>
         <meta-data />
      </activity-alias>
      <service>
         <intent-filter> Something goes here </intent-filter>
         <meta-data/>
      </service>
      <receiver>
         <intent-filter> Something goes here </intent-filter>
         <meta-data />
      </receiver>
      <provider>
         <grant-uri-permission />
         <meta-data />
         <path-permission />
      </provider>
      <uses-library />
   </application>
</manifest>
```

Gradle Build File

Based on Build.gradle (Module: app), in this file we can specify the minimum version for our app to be compiled and run on, minimum supported version and target version, the app version code and the app version name, proguard file, and dependencies.

There are a few build.gradle file make sure you access the one in app module
- AndroidStudioProjects\AppName\app see Fig. 2.16.

```
apply plugin: 'com.android.application'

android {
    compileSdkVersion 23
    // Specifies build tool version
    buildToolsVersion "24.0.0"

    defaultConfig {
        applicationId "com.alkathirikhalid.audiorecorder"
        // Specifies minimum supported version
        minSdkVersion 16
        // specifies the target version
        targetSdkVersion 23
        // The version code increases by 1 integer
        versionCode 1
        // Human readable and expressed as 1.1 or any value
        versionName "1.0"
    }
    buildTypes {
        release {
            minifyEnabled false
            proguardFiles getDefaultProguardFile('proguard-android.txt'), 'proguard-
rules.pro'
        }
    }
}

dependencies {
    compile fileTree(dir: 'libs', include: ['*.jar'])
    testCompile 'junit:junit:4.12'
    // Specifies the support version
    compile 'com.android.support:appcompat-v7:23.4.0'
}
```

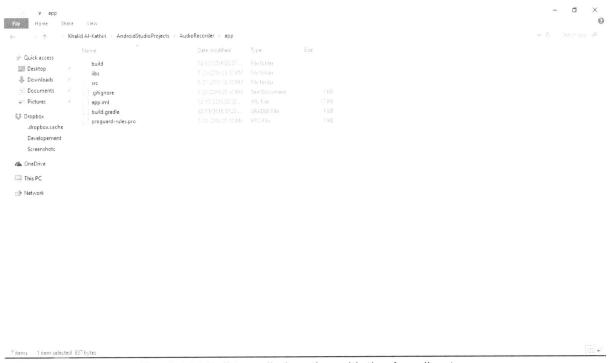

Fig. 2.16 | Build.gradle location with the App directory

Android Architecture

Android is made up to five major layers Fig. 2.17. the Linux Kernel is the basic hardware abstraction layer, here the Linux Operating system provides the drivers for the device peripherals such as Display, Camera and so forth hence Android platform provides the security of the Linux kernel, as well as a secure inter-process communication facility to enable secure communication between applications running in different processes. These security features at the Operating System level ensure that even native code is constrained by the Application Sandbox.

The Android Library package is a set of code libraries such as:
- Surface Manager: provide access to the display
- Media Framework: handles audio, video formats
- Libwebcore: A webkit browser engine
- SGL: 2D library
- OpenGL|ES: 3D library
- Freetype: Font library
- SQLite: Relational Database library

All these provide backward compatible versions of Android framework APIs as well as features that are only available through the library APIs This means that. each Support Library is backward compatible to a specific Android API level.

The Android Runtime is made up of core libraries *android.jar* and *Dalvik Virtual Machine* or *ART* for Android 4.4 and above, DVM is suitable for mobile devices which have limitation in terms of memory and processing power as opposed to Java Virtual Machine also referred as JVM which runs on common computers and laptops. Dalvik is the process virtual machine a software that runs the apps on Android devices. Hence it is an integral part of Android, which is typically used on mobile devices such as mobile phones and tablet computers as well as more recently on embedded devices such as smart TVs and media streamers.

There is a difference between JVM and DVM as programs are commonly written in Java and compiled to bytecode. They are then converted from Java Virtual Machine compatible .class files to Dalvik compatible .dex commonly known as Dalvik Executable files before installation on a device.

The Application Framework is a full set of services built in Java, example such as "Views System" and "Windows Manager" which are basic display elements, all applications that we are going to build are going to directly interact with this layer.

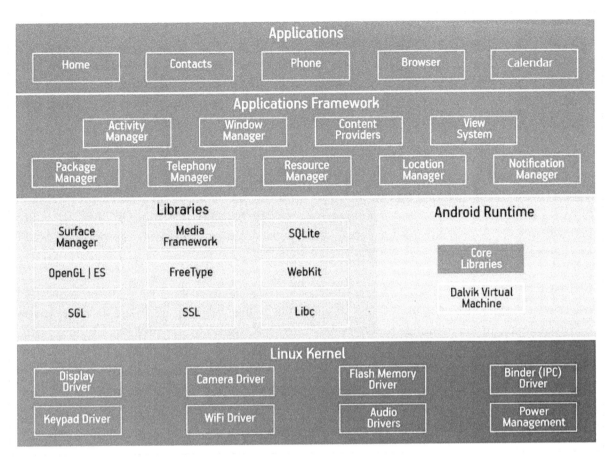

Fig. 2.17 | Android Architecture

The Linux Kernel

Android platform is based on the Linux kernel. Android Runtime (ART) previously Dalvik Virtual Machine (DVM) relies on the Linux kernel for functionalities such as threading and memory management. It also allows Android to take advantage of key security features and allows 3rd party device manufacturers to develop hardware drivers for a well-known kernel which is Linux as it has existed for quite a while with a huge developer community support.

Hardware Abstraction Layer

This provides standard interfaces that expose device hardware capabilities to the higher-level Java API framework. It consists of multiple library modules, and each of which implements an interface for a specific type of hardware component, example the camera or Bluetooth module. When a framework API makes a call to access device hardware, the Android system loads the library module for that hardware component.

Android Runtime

For devices running Android version 5.0 (API level 21) or higher, each app runs in its own process and with its own instance of the Android Runtime (ART). ART is written to run multiple virtual machines on low-memory devices by executing DEX files, a bytecode format designed especially for Android that's optimized for minimal memory footprint. Build toolchains, such as Jack, compile Java sources into DEX bytecode, which can run on the Android platform. Some of the major features of ART include the following:

- Ahead-of-time (AOT) and just-in-time (JIT) compilation
- Optimized garbage collection (GC)
- Better debugging support, including a dedicated sampling profiler, detailed diagnostic exceptions and crash reporting, and the ability to set watchpoints to monitor specific fields

Prior to Android version 5.0 (API level 21), Dalvik was the Android runtime. If your app runs well on ART, then it should work on Dalvik as well, but the reverse may not be true. Android also includes a set of core runtime libraries that provide most of the functionality of the Java programming language, including some Java 8 language features, that the Java API framework uses.

Native C/C++ Libraries

Many core Android system components and services, such as ART and HAL, are built from native code that require native libraries written in C and C++. The Android platform provides Java framework APIs to expose the functionality of some of these native libraries to apps. For example, you can access OpenGL ES through the Android framework's Java OpenGL API to add support for drawing and manipulating 2D and 3D graphics in your app. If you are developing an app that requires C or C++ code, you can use the Android NDK to access some of these native platform libraries directly from your native code.

Java API Framework

The entire feature-set of the Android OS is available to you through APIs written in the Java language. These APIs form the building blocks you need to create Android apps by simplifying the reuse of core, modular system components and services, which include the following:

- A rich and extensible View System you can use to build an app's UI, including lists, grids, text boxes, buttons, and even an embeddable web browser
- A Resource Manager, providing access to non-code resources such as localized strings, graphics, and layout files
- A Notification Manager that enables all apps to display custom alerts in the status bar
- An Activity Manager that manages the lifecycle of apps and provides a common navigation backstack
- Content Providers that enable apps to access data from other apps, such as the Contacts app, or to share their own data

This provides developers with full access to the same framework APIs that Android system apps uses.

System Apps

Android comes with a set of core apps for email, SMS messaging, calendars, internet browsing, contacts, and more. Apps included with the platform have no special status among the apps the user chooses to install. So a third-party app can become the user's default web browser, SMS messenger, or even the default keyboard (some exceptions apply, such as the system's Settings app). The system apps function both as apps for users and to provide key capabilities that developers can access from their own app. For example, if your app would like to deliver an SMS message, you don't need to build that functionality yourself, you can instead invoke whichever SMS app is already installed to deliver a message to the recipient you specify.

Android Activity Lifecycle

Android Activity goes through a lifecycle with a series of seven callback methods Fig. 2.18. Which allows a developer to specify what need to happen when the Activity goes through its life cycle.

onCreate

This is the first callback and called when the activity is first created, You must implement the onCreate() method to perform basic application startup logic that should happen only once for the entire life of the activity. For example, your implementation of onCreate() should define the user interface and possibly instantiate some class-scope variables.

onStart

This callback is called when the activity becomes visible to the user

onResume

This is called when the user starts interacting with the application, remains in the Resumed state until something occurs to change that, such as when a phone call is received, the user navigates to another activity, or the device screen turns off.

onPause

The paused activity does not receive user input and cannot execute any code and called when the current activity is being paused and the previous activity is being resumed, the activity is still partially visible, but most often is an indication that the user is leaving the activity and it will soon enter the Stopped state. You should usually use this method to:

- Check if the activity is visible; if it is not, stop animations or other ongoing actions that could consume CPU. Beginning with Android 7.0, a paused app might be running in multi-window mode. In this case, you would not want to stop animations or video playback.
- Commit unsaved changes, but only if users expect such changes to be permanently saved when they leave such as a draft email
- Release system resources, such as broadcast receivers, handles to sensors like GPS, or any resources that may affect battery life while your activity is paused and the user does not need them.

onStop

This callback is called when the activity is no longer visible, you should perform heavy-load shutdown operations during this method such as saving data to database, you should release almost all resources that are not needed while the user is not using it. Once your activity is stopped, the system might destroy the instance if it needs to recover system memory. In some extreme cases, the system might simply kill your app process without calling the activity's final onDestroy() callback, so it is very important you use this method to release resources that might leak memory.

onDestroy

This callback is called before the activity is destroyed by the system

onRestart

This callback is called when the activity restarts after stopping it

In many instances you probably would not need to implement all the lifecycle methods, but it is important to understand each one and implement those that ensure your app behaves the way users expect such as:

- Does not crash when a user receives a call or switches to another app while using your app
- It would not consume valuable system resources when the user is not actively using it
- Users do not lose their progress if they leave your app and return to it at a later time
- It would not crash or when the screen rotates between landscape and portrait orientation

Resumed: The activity is in the foreground and the user can interact with it

Paused: The activity is partially obscured by another activity. The paused activity does not receive user input and cannot execute any code

Stopped: The activity is completely hidden and not visible to the user; it is considered to be in the background. While stopped, the activity instance and all its state information such as member variables is retained, but it cannot execute any code

The "Created" and "Started" are transient and the system quickly moves from them to the next state by calling the next lifecycle callback method. That is, after the system calls onCreate(), it quickly calls onStart(), which is quickly followed by onResume(). Hence note that the application while running an in foreground it is in Resume state and initial coding such as assigning variable or objects to be create happens onCreate(). It is also a good idea to release resources onPause() by calling the release() method on applications using resources such as a camera.

TIP #15: Remember poorly written Android Application will result in poor performance and unnecessary processing usage and battery power drainage, if your app uses hardware such as GPS ensure to release onPause() as to avoid unnecessary power usage.

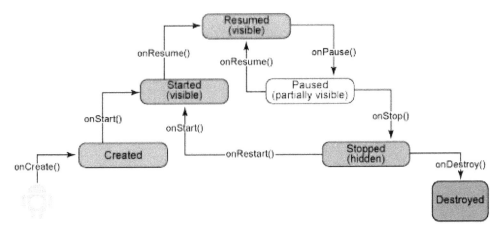

Fig. 2.18 | Android Activity Lifecycle

Let us now have a look at the full blown example on an application with all the Android Activity method callbacks and inline comment for further elaboration and explanation.

TIP #16: Remember when writing your code just like in JAVA prefer static methods over Objects allocation if and when multiple instances are not required, as it takes up memory, use local variables over class variable as these get created and destroyed when the method is called and executed.

```
package com.alkathinkhatid.hellowond;

import android.os.Bundle;
import android.app.Activity;

public class MainActivity extends Activity {

    @Override
    public void onCreate(Bundle savedInstanceState) {
        super.onCreate(savedInstanceState);
        setContentView(R.layout.activity_main);
    }

    @Override
    protected void onStart() {
        super.onStart();
    }

    @Override
    protected void onResume() {
        super.onResume();
    }

    @Override
    protected void onPause() {
        super.onPause();
    }

    @Override
    protected void onStop() {
        super.onStop();
    }

    @Override
    public void onDestroy() {
        super.onDestroy();
    }
}
```

Knowledge Check

1. Would you build an App using Android version 2.1? Explain why you would or you would not.
2. Android KitKat is what version of Android?
3. Is it possible to build Android Apps through Command line?
4. Where would you find resources directory for your app while coding in Android Studio
5. Is it important for the App directory folders to named accordingly or developers can name them randomly?
6. When and why would you used support libraries such as: android.support.v7.app.AppCompatActivity
7. Name other View Groups that you are aware off in Android
8. Where would you look to know which Activity will be the start of the App
9. Explain briefly Android Architecture
10. Explain briefly the Activity Lifecycle and what happens in the callback methods such as onResume()

Lab Exercise

1. Include all the life cycle callback in your first App
2. Run your application
    a. What are your observation?
    b. Did anything happen?
3. Change Activity to AppCompatActivity or vice versa
    a. What are your observation?
    b. Did anything happen?
4. Change your gradle build file minimum sdk version with a version higher than your AVD or Mobile device, run the application again
    a. What are your observation?
    b. Did anything happen?
5. Within dependencies comment out compile 'com.android.support:appcompat-v7:23.4.0' while your activity extends AppCompatActivity
    a. What are your observation?
    b. Did anything happen?

Chapter 3

Introduction

Here we are going to see source code version control, apps and code beyond first app, we are going to cover and how to apply in details about layouts, views such as buttons, edit text etc. and how to build Notepad App which is based on Notepad application sample provided by Android.

Source Control

Source version control is a system that records changes to a file or set of files (whole application) over time so that you can recall specific versions or changes later, as briefly mentioned in Chapter 1, Installing Android Studio Fig. 1.4. and Fig. 1.6.

Here we are going to use a source version control, to keep track of the changes made to our code and the app as a whole, this is crucial to be in the position to keep track and see the changes evolve and also to revert back to preferred or previous working version just in case things don't work out as planned.

When working alone or as a group you would like to know what and where a piece of code was added or modified last, and be in a position to determine what changes had taken effect overtime. With a source version control, it is possible to revert to any saved or committed version of our app.

Android Studio Version Control

There are currently six supported version control in Android Studio Fig. 3.1. When writing this book, namely:
- GitHub
- CVS
- Git
- Google Cloud
- Mercurial
- Subversion

TIP #17: Any one of the version control above will work just fine, it is ideally for beginners to use the GUI version control system rather than the console version control system, as it will take time for beginners to master most to all of the command.

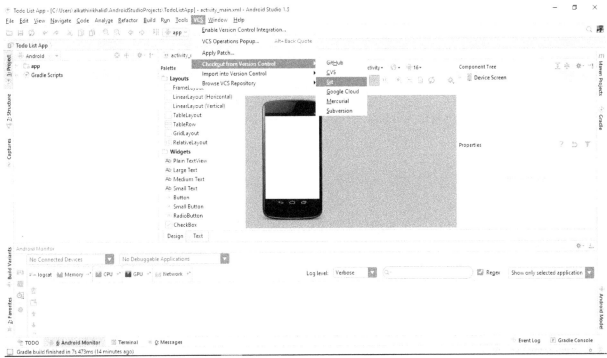

Fig. 3.1. Version Control Systems

Git

Git is a free and open source distributed version control system which was designed to handle small to large projects, it is quite fast and efficiency. Its advantages are that it is easy to learn and has a tiny footprint which makes it fast performance. It also the core for SCM tools like:

- Subversion
- CVS
- Perforce
- ClearCase
- etc.

Installation and setup

There are plenty of Git flavor but they work the same except the command line for Unix and windows system is a bit different, all Git flavor version cater for the type of operating system it's being installed in.

The main website for Git which offers multiple OS support such as Mac, Windows, Solaris and Linux is:

- https://git-scm.com/

While the link for Git for Windows OS support is:

- https://git-for-windows.github.io/

Download and running the Git you want to install, the website will detect your operating system and if your computer is 32 or 64 bit, ensure the right version is downloaded, here we will be using the first link above, see Fig. 3.2.

If you are running on windows and want to pass Git commands in your windows command prompt, ensure *'Use Git from the Windows Command Prompt'* is selected Fig. 3.3. You may leave the rest of the setting as default.

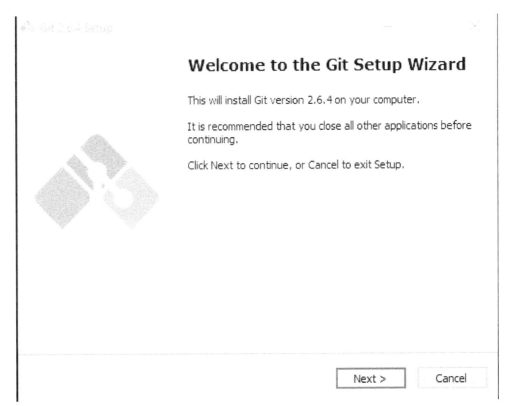

Fig. 3.2 | Git Installation

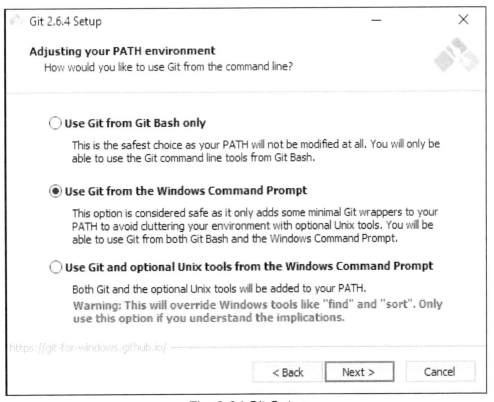

Fig. 3.3 | Git Setup

Git Commands

In this book we are going to cover some git commands briefly as we commence with the course such as:

- git --version
- git init
- git add FILE
- git add .
- git add * EXTENSION
- git commit -m 'MESSAGE'
- git clone URL
- git status
- git log
- git help

For a further comprehensive guide, tutorial and books, you may have a look at the below links:

- https://git-scm.com/doc
- https://git-scm.com/book/

Git installation verification

In order to verify that the installation was successful ensure you did enable the option in Fig. 3.3. if you are going to use Git in windows command prompt, this option basically adds a path to your system to interpret Git commands Fig. 3.4.

Type git --version in the command prompt to verify the Git version installed in your system Fig. 3.5.

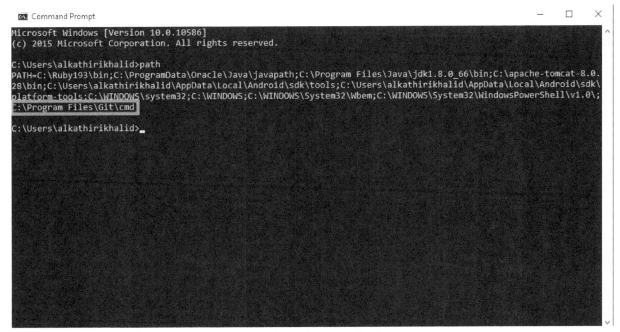

Fig. 3.4 | System Path

Fig. 3.5 | Git Version

Android Studio Git Setup

Once you have completed Git installation and setup, it is easy to locate, set and use it in Android Studio, click the File menu in Android Studio:

- File > Settings > Version Control > Git

Ensure path to Git executable should be pointing to the directory where Git command resides as depicted in Fig. 3.6. in this case:

- C:\Program Files\Git\cmd\git.exe

Click the 'Test' button to test whether Git is executable or not, you should get a confirmation window as seen in Fig. 3.7. This basically runs git --version command in the graphical user interface (GUI) and returns the git version as seen 2.6.4, same process as depicted in Fig. 3.5. but in Android Studio Integrated Development Environment (IDE).

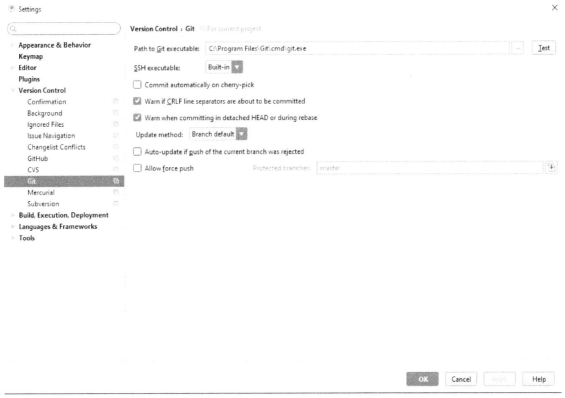

Fig. 3.6 | Android Studio Git Setup

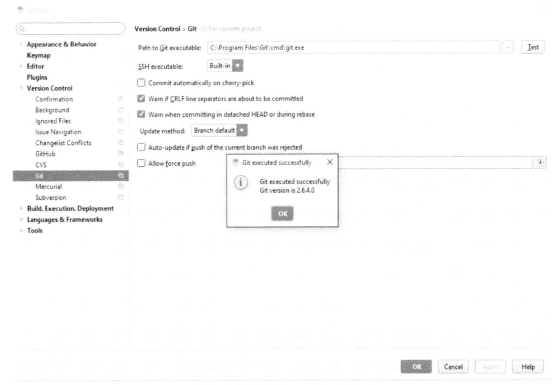

Fig. 3.7 | Git Execution Test

Notepad App

We are going to build a simple Notepad application that takes data from user and lists them in the view, open up Android Studio and create a new module (is a single app) in the first App Project Fig. 3.8. to Fig. 3.9:

1. Select Phone & Tablet Module and click Next
2. Give application name Notepad App, set minimum SDK API 16 Android 4.1 and click Next
3. Select Blank Activity and click Next
4. Leave the default values and click Finish

or create a totally new project (is a collection of apps) based on the settings (1-4) above. See *How to Start Android App Development* in *Chapter 2*.

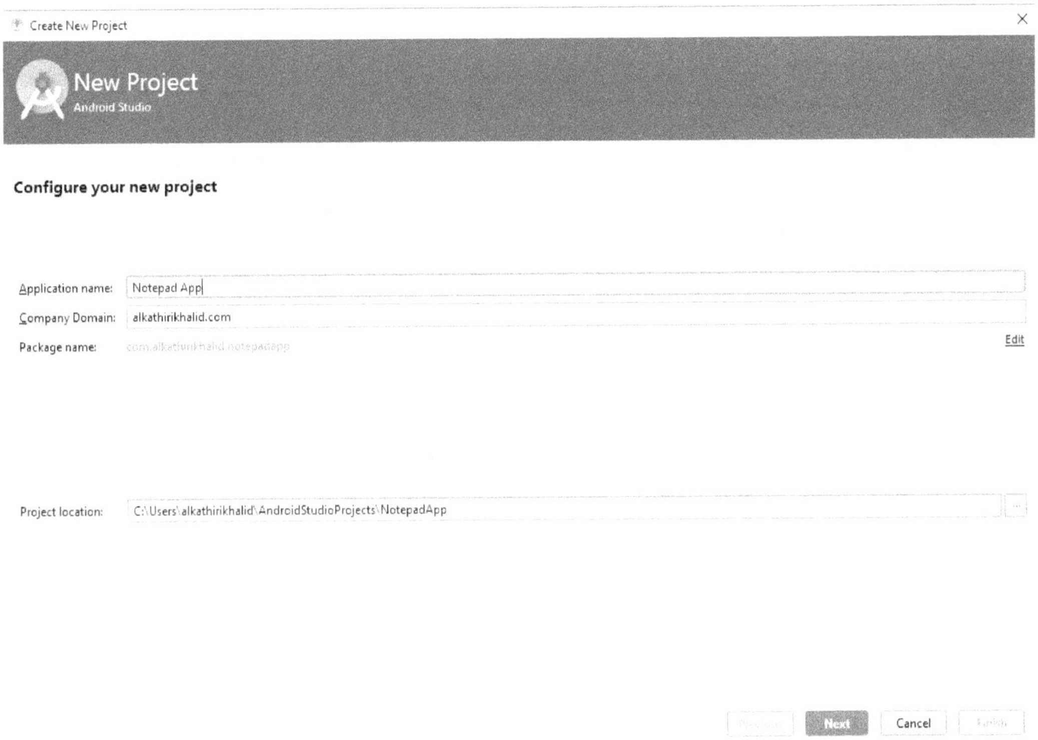

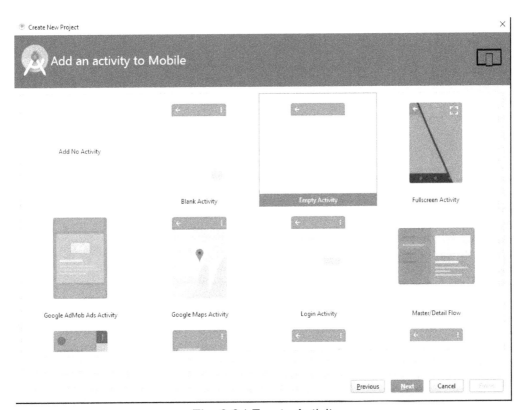

Fig. 3.8 | Notepad App

Fig. 3.9 | Empty Activity

Ensure you change to:
- Activity Name: NoteEdit
- Layout Name: note_edit

Android Studio will create a skeleton application with the above setting Fig. 3.10. Let us now change the default launcher image (ic_launcher) found in res/mipmap...
1. Right click app in Android studio and select image asset Fig. 3.11.
2. Specify Asset Type as Launcher Icons
3. Specify Image file for the location of the image, click OK, Next and Finish

TIP #18: When you specify an Image as an Asset ensure you select an image with high resolution such as 512 X 512 this will allow Android Studio to resize this image asset to support a broad list of devices with different screen sizes and resolution, once a user runs your app on their device Android will automatically pick an asset image that suits their screen size and resolution.

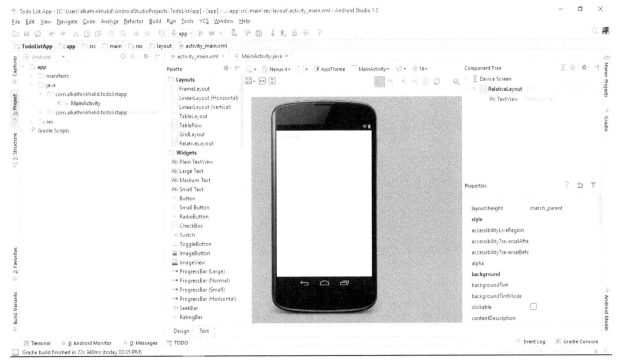

Fig. 3.10. | Skeletal Notepad App

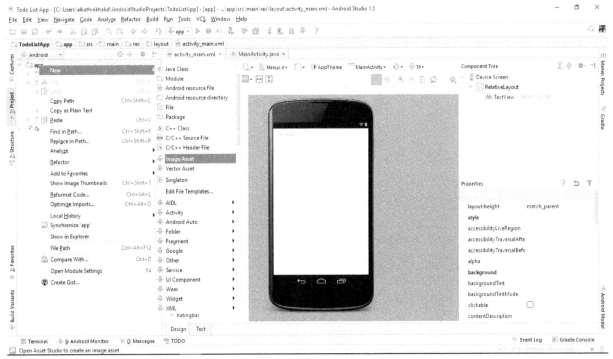

Fig. 3.11. | Image Asset

Launcher Icon

The launcher icon has its predefined size to support a variety of screen sizes and resolution and each is place in its appropriate folder res/mipmap-<h/m/x/xx/xxx>hdpi/

- 48 × 48 (mdpi)
- 72 × 72 (hdpi)
- 96 × 96 (xhdpi)
- 144 × 144 (xxhdpi)
- 192 × 192 (xxxhdpi)
- 512 × 512 (Google Play store)

It is imperative to supply the right image size in the right folder. You could alternately generate the icon launcher from Android UI utilities online generator:

- http://romannurik.github.io/AndroidAssetStudio/
- You can also set a clipart as an icon, set a clipart as our Notepad App launcher icon, see Fig. 3.12.

Impact on View

If you do not supply an image with high resolution but instead a lower one, the image will appear blur and your app won't look nice on devices with a higher screen size and resolution.

Impact on Performance

On the other hand, if you supply just one image without generating the rest into the appropriate res/mipmap-<h/m/x/xx/xxx>hdpi/ this will force the user device to generate and render its own suitable resource base on the one resource you provide, so every time Android will be force to calculate, generate and render an asset this will consume processing power and time and in turn impact your app performance.

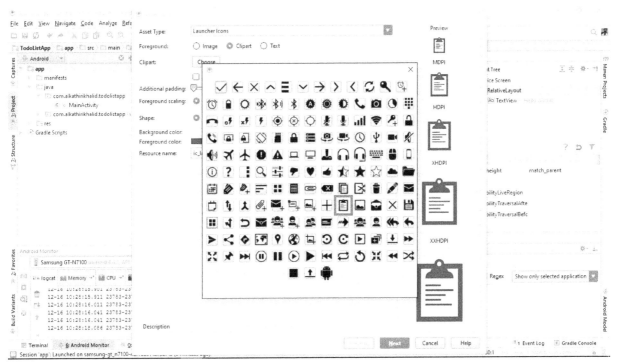

Fig 3.12. | Clipart as Launcher icon

Notepad App Git Setup

Here we will setup git integration to our notepad Application, head on and click:

- VCS > Enable Version Control Integration as depicted in Fig. 3.13.

And select a version control system of your choice with the project root of your app and click OK, in this book we are going to use Git as depicted in Fig. 3.14.

It is wise and safe to use a version control system to keep track of your app progress and be in the position to revert in case of rogue code or hard to spot bugs and also from protection of losing your entire code in case of a hard disk failure, this can be achieved by backing up or keep in sync your local source control to a remote location such as a pc/storage in your network or in the cloud.

Cloud source control as mentioned in 'Android Studio Version Control'. The most common are GitHub and Bitbucket which offer some free storage depending on their terms and conditions.

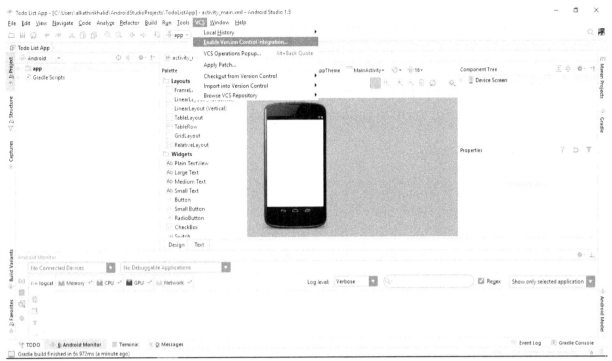

Fig.3.13 | Enable Version Control Integration

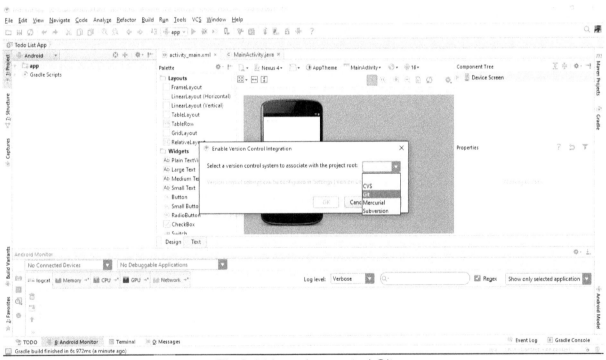

Fig.3.14 | version control Git

Add files to be tracked by Git

After associating our project root, Git will scan and keep track of all the files list with in the project root and mark the files to be added for tracking as red in Android Studio, as seen in Fig. 3.15. note_edit.xml, NoteEdit.java, AndroidManifest.xml etc.

We will need to add the files Fig. 3.16. In Order to be tracked by Git, head to:
- VCS > Git > +Add
- Or Simply press Ctrl+Alt+A

This is a useful technique for a source version control to allow the developer the flexibility to add or remove files to be tracked, such temporary files or IDE generated files can be excluded as they are not part of the actual source code rather than the project setup instructions for the developer or for the specific IDE in use for this example is Android Studio auto generated files can be ignore as we will see later in Fig. 3.18. untracked files.

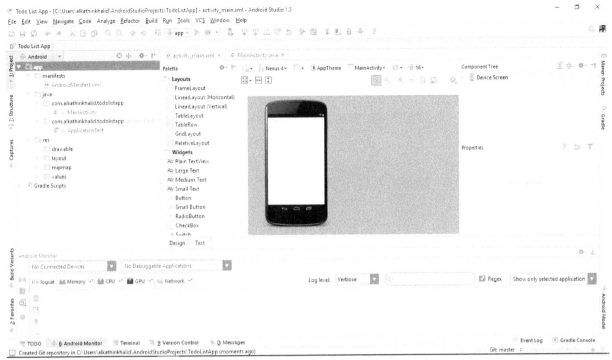

Fig. .3.15 | Untracked files appear red

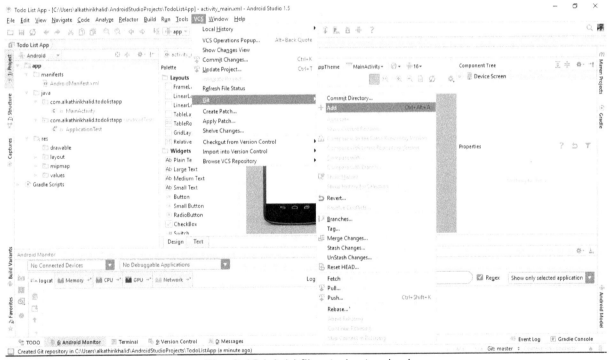

Fig. 3.16 | Add files to be tracked

List tracked and untracked files by Git

All the tracked file now will change color from red too green, as a sign of tracked files within Android Studio Environment as depicted in Fig. 3.17.

Let us verify the tracked and untracked file list as seen in Fig. 3.18. Using Command Prompt in windows run:

- git status

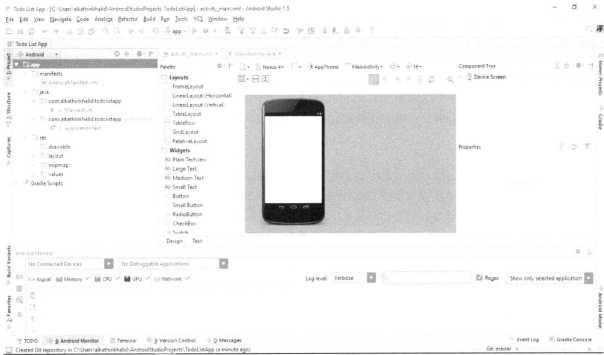

Fig. 3.17 | Tracked files appear green

Fig. 3.18 | List of tracked and untracked files respectively

Before Developing

Now we have done the version control setup. Learned and applied some of the Git commands both from command line and in Android Studio, we are all set to begin, but before we jump ahead into coding, let us learn to do coding the right way and that is to follow Systems Development Life Cycle (SDLC), a stands for software development lifecycle. It is essentially a series of steps, or phases, that provide a model for the development and lifecycle management of an app or any piece of software Fig. 3.19.

The series of steps might vary from one project to another depending on the model for developing or implementing the requirements to meet the needs of the stakeholders, managing resources and other factors that will determine the app or software delivery, below is a common basic SDLC:

- Planning > Analysis > Design > Implementation > Support

Each step will have a series of tasks and these steps might or might not be dependent on the previous steps or phase. The phases are clearly defined with distinct work phases which are used by systems software engineers to plan, design, build, test, and deliver the app or software.

In this book we are going to start with the Planning phase by evaluation of present Notepad apps, information gathering, feasibility study and request approval, since the app we are building is for learning purposes and is of very small project with minimum requirement the information provided here is to expose you on real life work environments.

A number of SDLC models have been created example such as: waterfall, fountain, spiral, rapid prototyping Fig. 3.20, incremental etc. which are not the objective of this book but simply to give you a better approach on how to build real life applications that is functional, usable and appealing to your target audience.

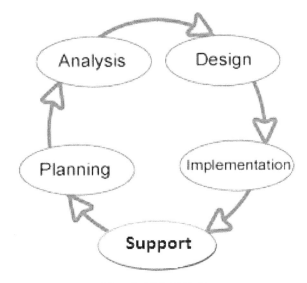

Fig. 3.19 | SDLC

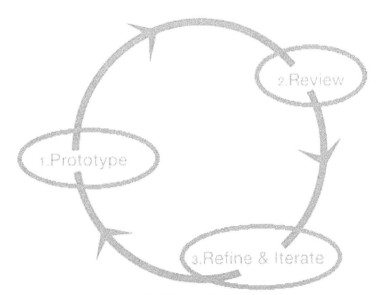

Fig. 3.20 | Rapid Prototyping

Planning

We will begin by Planning where we describe features and operations in detail, with screen layouts, pseudocode and other documentation if necessary. We are going to jump right ahead into our screen layouts using the basic tool would be a pen and paper but for professional craftsmanship we use specific software that allows us to visual foresee a look of how our app will look and using predefined common shapes that are easy to drag and drop to plan your screen layout and that is by using Wireframe.

Wireframe

Wireframe are basically software tools that allows a system designer or architect to do mockups these mockups can be a series of image each representing a screen such as http://lucidchart.com/ or a compiled image into a video to demonstrate the user flow from one screen to the other such as https://proto.io/ and many others.

Our application will have two screens one is to show the available note Fig. 3.21, in a list format within each line and the other is the actual content of the note which allows the user to add or edit, when a user selects a note title in the list available in the first screen the second screen with allow user to see or change the content Fig. 3.22.

User Actions Overall - Empty App

First Screen

- Add a note by clicking Add Note button
- Open / Delete a Note

Second Screen

- Create / Read / Update Note
- Edit Note Title and Notes

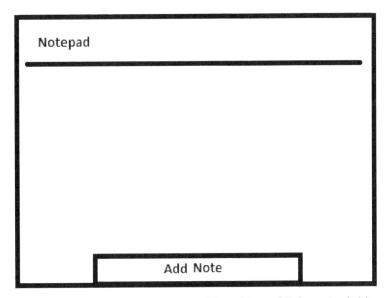

Fig. 3.21 | Screen 1 - Empty List - User Clicks + to Add

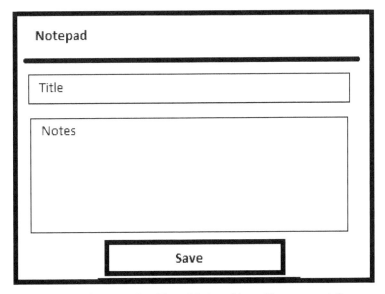

Fig 3.22 | Screen 2 - New Note - User Types and Save

To fully demonstrate the whole actions a user can do we will need to add more screens or scenarios to have a better clear understanding of what the app flow is and how it is supposed to function, the main aim for wire framing is clarity to all that are going to be involved in the application development, a clear concise the ins and outs of an app and to achieve that proper documentation is involved.

We are going to address the functionality if and when the app has data and presented in a list format Fig. 3.23, the previous functionality is still available with an option now of being able to select a Note in the list and either Add / Edit / Save or Delete Fig. 3.24, so we are going to point out just the new available function in the app in a scenario where it is not empty.

User Actions - Unempty App

First Screen

- Select a Note from a list

Second Screen

- Add / Edit / Save / Delete Note contents

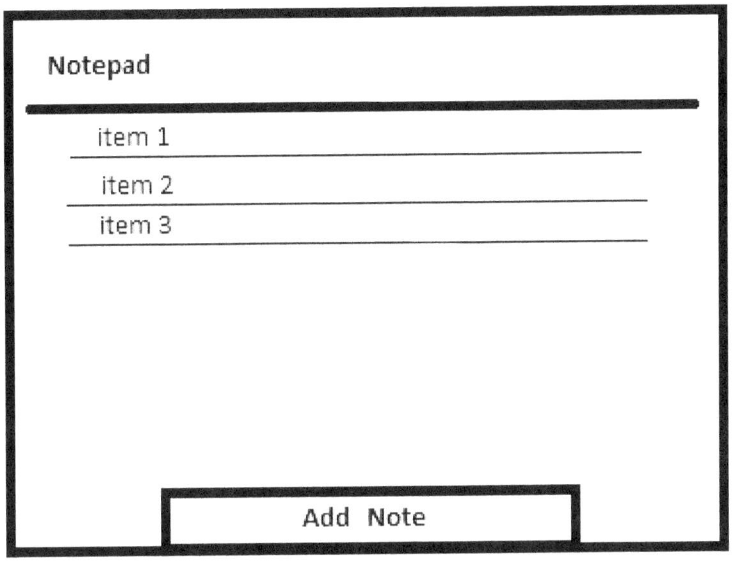

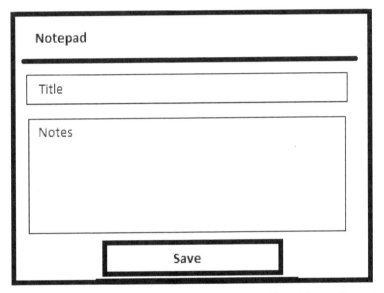

Fig. 3.23 | Screen 1 - Note List - User Selects item 1

Fig. 3.24 | Screen 2 - Note - User Views / Edit / Save item 1

Rather than the user to select an item, then open the second screen and perform an action, we can simplify and present the action of the first screen by using another trigger which is a long press Fig. 3.25 notice the dot we will elaborate on that shortly, so long as the user long press the item desired for the particular action, this in turn will reduce the number of steps a user must perform in order to complete a task Fig. 3.26.

#TIP 19: Denote user interactions / gestures with the screen by providing extract information in your wireframe such as a circle to represent a tap or click, double circle for a double tap, a dark circle for a long press, to give a better understanding of how the app works and how the user is intended to interact with the app, this is very useful for the programmer who is going to build the app to know what action gesture should trigger a desirable action etc.

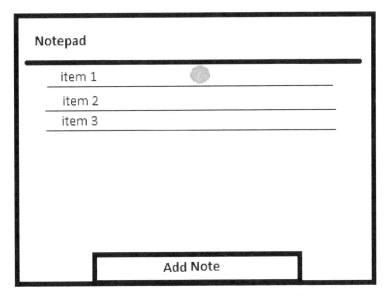

Fig. 3.25 | Screen 1 - Note List - User Long Press item 1

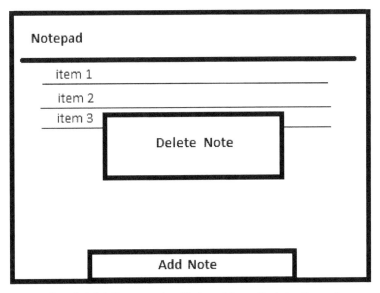

Fig. 3.26 | Screen 1 - Note - User Delete item 1

Wireframe Gestures presentation

We can further enhance our wireframe by including touch gestures to simulate user interaction with our app, as demonstrated previously Fig. 3.25. with a dot.

Depending on what you are working on or what interactions you are simulating, the notations, images and meaning may vary from one wireframe application to another including designer specification and taste, Fig. 3.27 are some of the common screen gestures. In our wireframe previously we just included a filled dot without an arrow to indicate a long press.

TIP #19: You can get a free wireframe GUI template for Android but make sure you follow the Android specification that is the Android Design Patterns, this will ensure usability of your app to your target audience that is Android users, an understood UI flow will ensure user familiarity with your app and make navigation and usage easy, this in turn will increasing the overall easy to use and intuitive in nature allowing users to use your app with little or no instructions at all, build something that users are familiar with to minimize / eliminate user frustration.

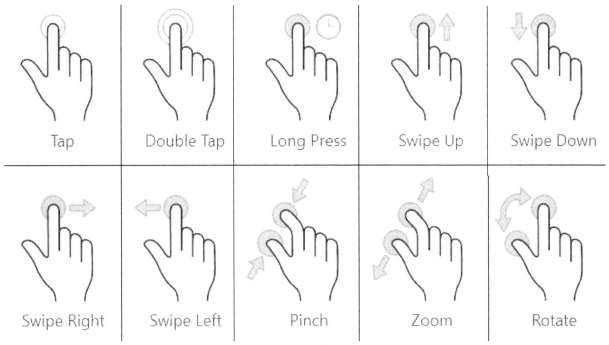

Fig. 3.27 | Common Screen gestures

Knowledge Check

1. Name some of the Source Control Version Systems available that you can use in Android Studio
2. What are the recommended links of Git for Mac or a PC?
3. What do you expect git --version command version to return?
4. What command would you use for git if you require some help or information for another command?
5. Is it really necessary a requirement to use a source version system?

Lab Exercise

1. Setup git in your development machine if you do not have already
2. Run Android Studio and Select Import an Android Code Sample
   a. You may select any code / application sample such as Bluetooth Chat
   b. Import and run the app you chose

Remember the lab exercise exposes you to the already rich pool of resources available to start coding or fully build an Android App.

Chapter 4

Introduction

Now that we have seen how to actually mock a UI using wireframe we are ready to begin building our app, there are a few approach on building application in software engineering and that is Top-down and bottom-up approach, we are not going to deal in details on the specifications on how one of them is carried out, in this chapter we will assume that all requirements are gathered and we are ready to build our app, we will follow the top-down approach for our Notepad App, most Android App development will use bottom-up approach, Android is a framework and almost all the necessary modules to build a functional app are provided within the framework.

To best distinguish the two approaches:
- Top down: You start with an existing domain model, and have complete freedom with respect to the design of the database schema.
- Bottom up: Begins with an existing database schema.

Our Notepad App will store and use data using SQLite database as it is the default database in Android, we will later need to design and construct a database access helper class which defines the CRUD operations for our Notepad App.

Building Notepad UI

We are going to construct the UI by renaming the existing xml layout file or completely create new one, here we will create our xml files namely: -
- note_edit (previously generated)
- notes_list
- notes_row

Go ahead and select your app folder and click
1. File > New > XML > Layout XML File Fig. 4.1.
2. Give it a name as note_edit
3. Root Tag LinearLayout
4. Click Finish
5. You will be prompted if you want to Add the File to Git, Select Yes Fig. 4.2.

Repeat the step 1-5 for the remaining two XML files namely notes_list and notes_row.

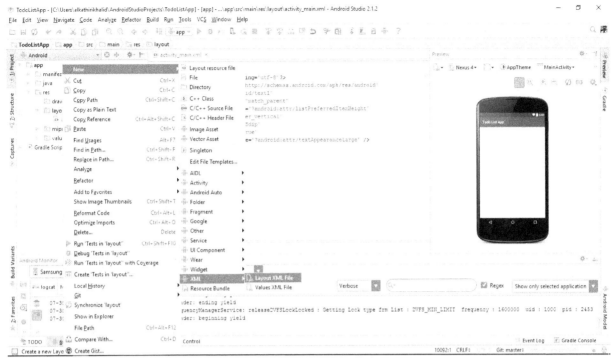

Fig. 4.1 | Creating Layout XML File

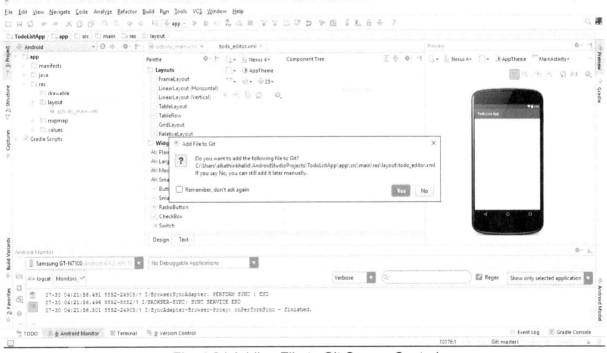

Fig. 4.2 | Adding File to Git Source Control

Note Edit

We will need to change the code for the xml file, the original file contains a view group of type linear layout and without any children or views, basically it's an empty holder without any views to display to the screen.

Original

```
<?xml version="1.0" encoding="utf-8"?>
<LinearLayout xmlns:android="http://schemas.android.com/apk/res/android"
    android:layout_width="match_parent"
    android:layout_height="match_parent">
</LinearLayout>
```

Modified

```
<?xml version="1.0" encoding="utf-8"?>
<LinearLayout xmlns:android="http://schemas.android.com/apk/res/android"
    android:layout_width="match_parent"
    android:layout_height="match_parent"
    android:orientation="vertical">

    <EditText
        android:id="@+id/title"
        android:layout_width="match_parent"
        android:layout_height="wrap_content"
        android:hint="Title" />

    <EditText
        android:id="@+id/body"
        android:layout_width="match_parent"
        android:layout_height="wrap_content"
        android:layout_gravity="center_horizontal"
        android:layout_weight="1"
        android:hint="Notes" />

    <Button
        android:id="@+id/save"
        style="?android:attr/buttonStyleSmall"
        android:layout_width="match_parent"
        android:layout_height="wrap_content"
        android:layout_gravity="center_horizontal"
        android:text="Save" />
</LinearLayout>
```

Explanation

Here we have added three objects that is two edit texts one for the title and the other for the contents, we have also added a button to save.

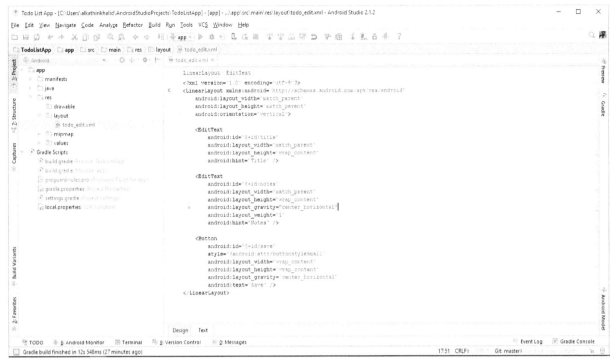

Fig. 4.3. | Modified note_edit.xml

Notes List

We will need to change the code for the xml file just like we have seen before, as the original file contains a view group of type linear layout and without any children or views, basically it's an empty holder without any views to display to the screen, we will remove the basic template generate code with our modified code.

Original

```xml
<?xml version="1.0" encoding="utf-8"?>
<LinearLayout xmlns:android="http://schemas.android.com/apk/res/android"
    android:layout_width="match_parent"
    android:layout_height="match_parent">
</LinearLayout>
```

Modified

```xml
<?xml version="1.0" encoding="utf-8"?>
<LinearLayout xmlns:android="http://schemas.android.com/apk/res/android"
    android:layout_width="match_parent"
    android:layout_height="match_parent"
    android:orientation="vertical">

    <TextView
        android:id="@+id/android:empty"
        android:layout_width="wrap_content"
        android:layout_height="wrap_content"
        android:text="Add Notes, the list is empty" />

    <ListView
        android:id="@+id/android:list"
        android:layout_width="wrap_content"
        android:layout_height="wrap_content" />
</LinearLayout>
```

Explanation

Here we have added a textview to notify user in the event where by data has never been added, and a listview to populate previous added data.

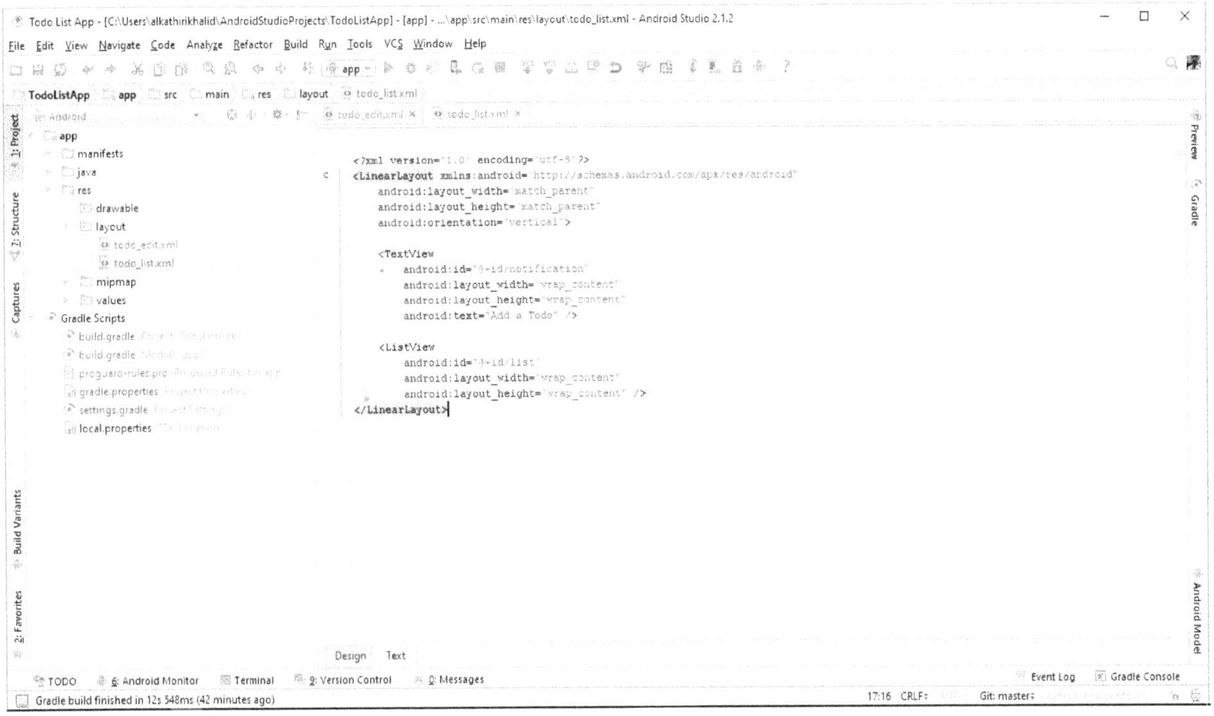

Fig. 4.4. | Modified notes_list.xml

Notes Row

As seen previously here we will change the code for the xml file just like before, as the original file contains a view group of type linear layout and without any children or views, basically it's an empty holder without any views to display to the screen, we will remove the basic template generate code with our modified code.

Original

```
<?xml version="1.0" encoding="utf-8"?>
<LinearLayout xmlns:android="http://schemas.android.com/apk/res/android"
    android:layout_width="match_parent"
    android:layout_height="match_parent">
</LinearLayout>
```

Modified

```
<?xml version="1.0" encoding="utf-8"?>
<TextView xmlns:android="http://schemas.android.com/apk/res/android"
    android:id="@+id/text"
    android:layout_width="wrap_content"
    android:layout_height="wrap_content"
    android:padding="10dp"
    android:textSize="20sp" />
```

Explanation

Here we are creating a textview to be used and presented as a row within the listview so as to show as individual items within the list.

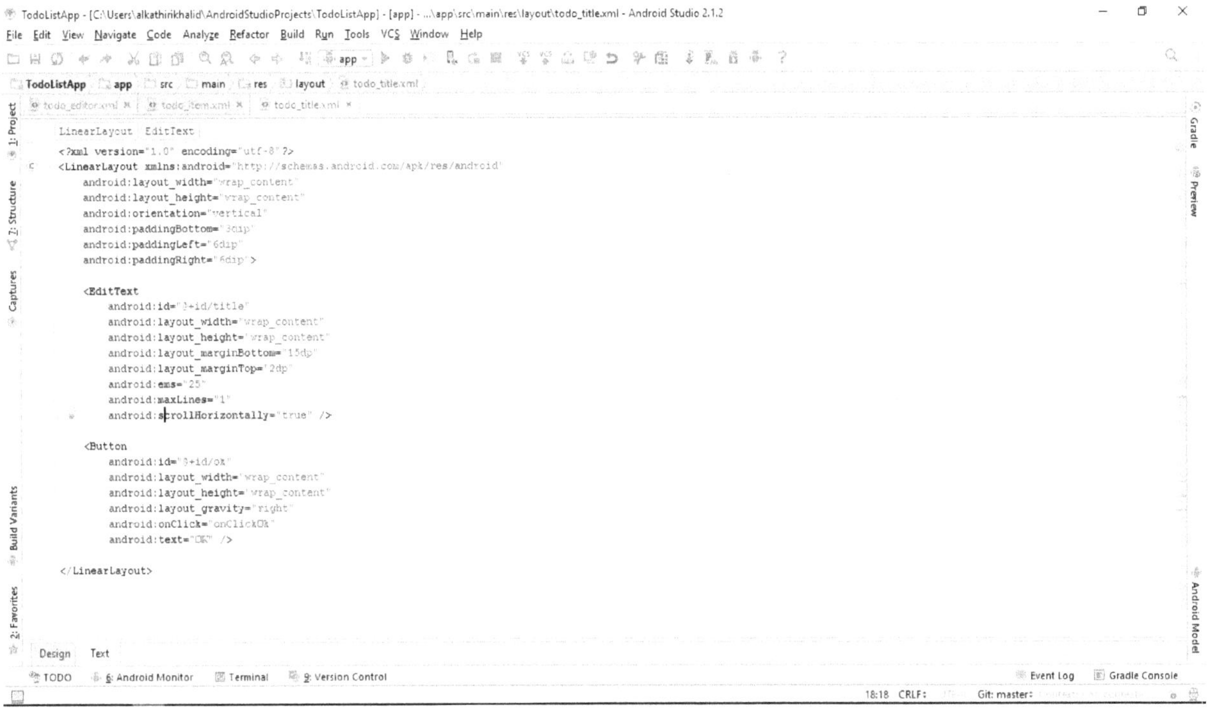

Fig. 4.5. | Modified notes_row.xml

Adding a Menu

A menu provides a number of functionality to the user that are not currently presented directly on the Activity Screen, hence this allows us to added more functions and features for the user to perform without distorting the Activity view with unnecessary view objects such as buttons. This is not required for our Notepad App.

Most of the time a menu is a collection of reusable functionality that are familiar, consistent and present from one activity to another or sometimes a specific type of functionality for a specific Activity, it all comes down to the application and what was the original design.

We will add a menu to our Notepad App
1. Right Click Res folder
2. Select New > Android Resource Directory > Fig. 4.6.
3. Within the New Resource Directory set the Resource Type to menu
4. Click OK Fig. 4.7.

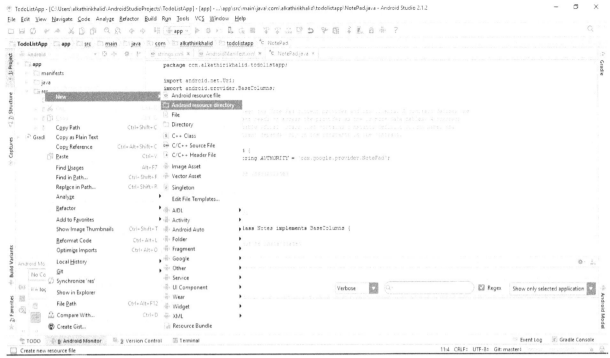

Fig. 4.6 | Android Resource Directory

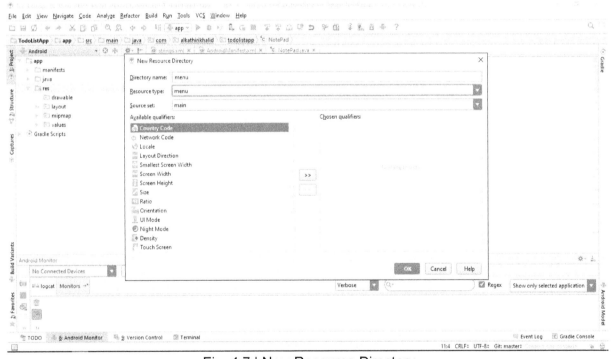

Fig. 4.7 | New Resource Directory

Now that we have an empty directory we can add an xml file for our menu, go ahead and add a Menu resource file in the resource directory we just created.

1. Right Click Menu directory
2. Select New > Menu resource File Fig. 4.8.
3. Give it a name editor_options
4. Leave Source set main
5. Leave Directory name menu
6. Click OK Fig. 4.9.

You will be prompted to Add the created file to Git, click OK.

Fig. 4.8 | Menu resource file

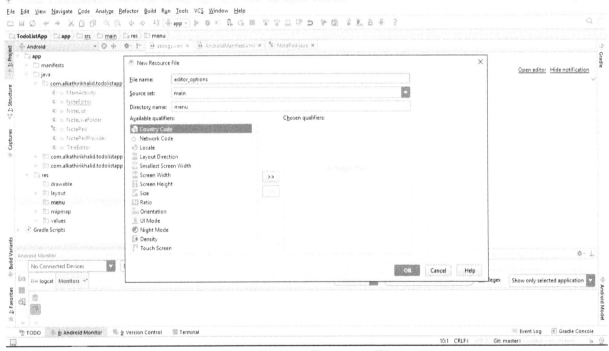

Fig. 4.9 | New Resource File

Our menu file is created without any items; you can easily start to insert items by using the shortcut Alt+Insert within the create file. Fig. 4.10.

editor_options.xml

```xml
<?xml version="1.0" encoding="utf-8"?>
<menu xmlns:android="http://schemas.android.com/apk/res/android">
    <item
        android:id="@+id/menu_add"
        android:icon="@drawable/ic_menu_add"
        android:title="Add Note" />
</menu>
```

We will need to have an icon to represent the menu button mentioned above add, we will use the in build Icons generator to create multiple icons for different dimensions:

1. Right Click Drawable
2. Select New Image Asset Fig. 4.11.

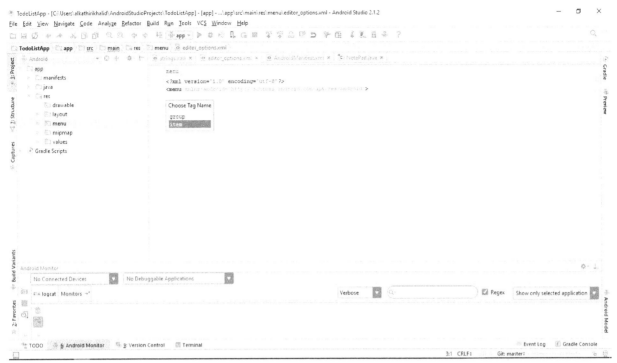

Fig. 4.10 | Click Alt+Insert to insert items

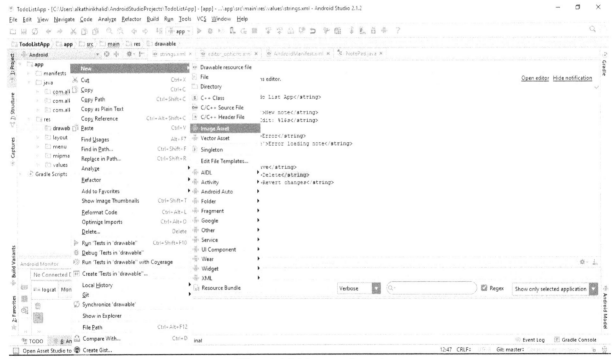

Fig. 4.11 | Image Asset

In the Generate Icon menu:
1. Select Action Bar and Tab Icons Fig. 4.12.
2. Give the image a name ic_menu-add
3. Click Clipart and select a plus sign +

You will be prompted to save the generate files to Git Fig. 4.13. click Ok.

After designing and creating the UI, we head on and created the backend which is purely java including the Database using SQLite in NoteDB.java which includes SQLite commands such as CREATE TABLE etc. As we have seen so far the main places of coding are:
- XML files for UI
- Java for Back End
- Manifest file for Permissions etc.

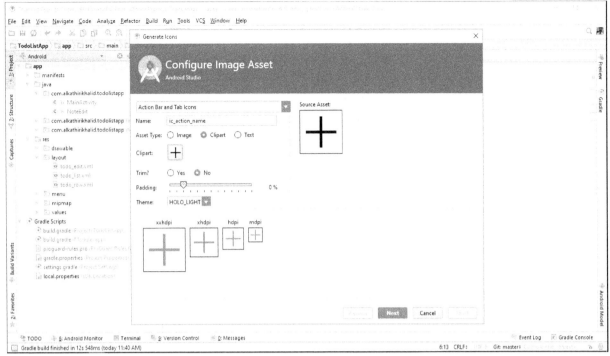

Fig. 4.12 | Configure Image Asset

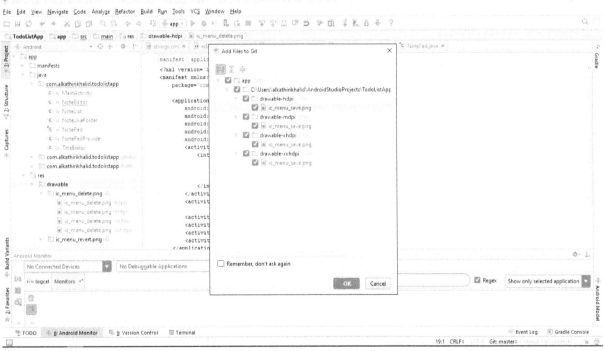

Fig. 4.13 | Add Files to Git

Building Notepad App Backend

We will now need to create the backend code that will react and work with our UI based on user interactions, that means we need to build our Java code in this case the activities that will handle the application and make the application interactive based on user actions on the UI.

Here we are going to create three classes that will handle our application, so that it can have backend functions.

- NoteEdit.java (previously generated)
- Notepad.java
- NotesDbAdapter.java

Go ahead and select your app folder and click

1. File > New > Activity > Empty Activity Fig. 4.14
2. Give it an Activity name as NoteEdit
3. Uncheck Generate Layout File as we have created them already
4. Package name leave default
5. Target source set main leave it default
6. Click Finish Fig. 4.15
7. You will be prompted if you want to Add the File to Git, Select Yes

Repeat the step 1-7 for the remaining two java files namely Notepad.java and NotesDbAdapter.java. Whereas NotesDbAdapter.java is not an Activity class rather than an adaptor that allows CRUD operation for our application.

TIP #20: By using the Android Studio inbuilt short cuts and creation wizard for i.e. an Activity it automatically adds an Activity entry in the AndroidManifest.xml file, rather than creating a Java class and extending it to An Activity you will manually need to state this in the manifest file.

```
</activity><activity android:name=".NoteEdit"></activity>
```

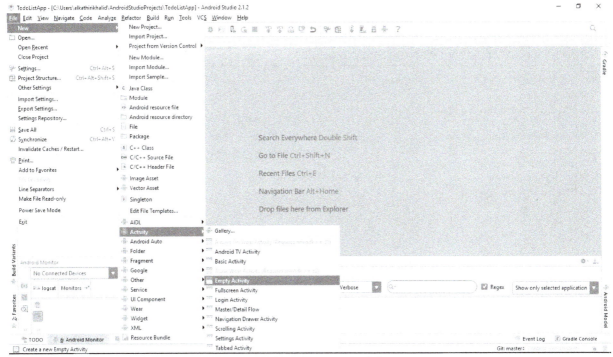

Fig. 4.14. | Empty Activity

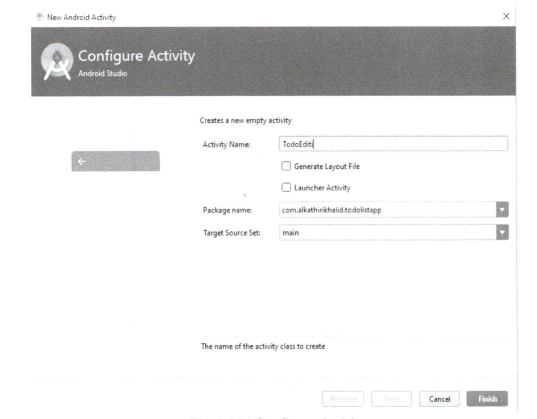

Fig. 4.15 | Configure Activity

Notes Db Adapter

Based on NotesDBAdapter class, this class will have the necessary SQLite statements to fully operate the Notepad App, as explained with in line comments.

```java
package com.alkathirikhalid.notepadapp;

import android.content.ContentValues;
import android.content.Context;
import android.database.Cursor;
import android.database.SQLException;
import android.database.sqlite.SQLiteDatabase;
import android.database.sqlite.SQLiteOpenHelper;
import android.util.Log;

/**
 * Simple notes database access helper class. Defines the basic CRUD operations
 * for the notepad example, and gives the ability to list all notes as well as
 * retrieve or modify a specific note.
 * <p/>
 * This has been improved from the first version of this tutorial through the
 * addition of better error handling and also using returning a Cursor instead
 * of using a collection of inner classes (which is less scalable and not
 * recommended).
 */
public class NotesDbAdapter {
    public static final String KEY_TITLE = "title";
    public static final String KEY_BODY = "body";
    public static final String KEY_ROWID = "_id";

    private static final String TAG = "NotesDbAdapter";
    private DatabaseHelper mDbHelper;
    private SQLiteDatabase mDb;

    /**
     * Database creation sql statement
     */
    private static final String DATABASE_CREATE =
            "create table notes (_id integer primary key autoincrement, "
                    + "title text not null, body text not null);";

    private static final String DATABASE_NAME = "data";
    private static final String DATABASE_TABLE = "notes";
    private static final int DATABASE_VERSION = 2;

    private final Context mCtx;

    private static class DatabaseHelper extends SQLiteOpenHelper {

        DatabaseHelper(Context context) {
            super(context, DATABASE_NAME, null, DATABASE_VERSION);
        }

        @Override
        public void onCreate(SQLiteDatabase db) {

            db.execSQL(DATABASE_CREATE);
        }

        @Override
        public void onUpgrade(SQLiteDatabase db, int oldVersion, int newVersion) {
            Log.w(TAG, "Upgrading database from version " + oldVersion + " to "
```

```
                    + newVersion + ", which will destroy all old data");
            db.execSQL("DROP TABLE IF EXISTS notes");
            onCreate(db);
        }
    }


    /**
     * Constructor - takes the context to allow the database to be
     * opened/created
     *
     * @param ctx the Context within which to work
     */
    public NotesDbAdapter(Context ctx) {
        this.mCtx = ctx;
    }


    /**
     * Open the notes database. If it cannot be opened, try to create a new
     * instance of the database. If it cannot be created, throw an exception to
     * signal the failure
     *
     * @return this (self reference, allowing this to be chained in an
     * initialization call)
     * @throws SQLException if the database could be neither opened or created
     */
    public NotesDbAdapter open() throws SQLException {
        mDbHelper = new DatabaseHelper(mCtx);
        mDb = mDbHelper.getWritableDatabase();
        return this;
    }


    public void close() {
        mDbHelper.close();
    }



    /**
     * Create a new note using the title and body provided. If the note is
     * successfully created return the new rowId for that note, otherwise return
     * a -1 to indicate failure.
     *
     * @param title the title of the note
     * @param body  the body of the note
     * @return rowId or -1 if failed
     */
    public long createNote(String title, String body) {
        ContentValues initialValues = new ContentValues();
        initialValues.put(KEY_TITLE, title);
        initialValues.put(KEY_BODY, body);

        return mDb.insert(DATABASE_TABLE, null, initialValues);
    }

    /**
     * Delete the note with the given rowId
     *
     * @param rowId id of note to delete
     * @return true if deleted, false otherwise
     */
    public boolean deleteNote(long rowId) {

        return mDb.delete(DATABASE_TABLE, KEY_ROWID + "=" + rowId, null) > 0;
    }
```

```java
    /**
     * Return a Cursor over the list of all notes in the database
     *
     * @return Cursor over all notes
     */
    public Cursor fetchAllNotes() {

        return mDb.query(DATABASE_TABLE, new String[]{KEY_ROWID, KEY_TITLE,
                KEY_BODY}, null, null, null, null, null);
    }


    /**
     * Return a Cursor positioned at the note that matches the given rowId
     *
     * @param rowId id of note to retrieve
     * @return Cursor positioned to matching note, if found
     * @throws SQLException if note could not be found/retrieved
     */
    public Cursor fetchNote(long rowId) throws SQLException {

        Cursor mCursor =

                mDb.query(true, DATABASE_TABLE, new String[]{KEY_ROWID,
                                KEY_TITLE, KEY_BODY}, KEY_ROWID + "=" + rowId, null,
                        null, null, null, null);
        if (mCursor != null) {
            mCursor.moveToFirst();
        }
        return mCursor;

    }


    /**
     * Update the note using the details provided. The note to be updated is
     * specified using the rowId, and it is altered to use the title and body
     * values passed in
     *
     * @param rowId id of note to update
     * @param title value to set note title to
     * @param body  value to set note body to
     * @return true if the note was successfully updated, false otherwise
     */
    public boolean updateNote(long rowId, String title, String body) {
        ContentValues args = new ContentValues();
        args.put(KEY_TITLE, title);
        args.put(KEY_BODY, body);

        return mDb.update(DATABASE_TABLE, args, KEY_ROWID + "=" + rowId, null) > 0;
    }
}
```

Note Edit

Based on NoteEdit.java class, this is the class that will actually handle the editing, by changing the layout to note_edit.xml, taking data from the title and body and inserting it into the database.

```java
package com.alkathirikhalid.notepadapp;

import android.app.Activity;
import android.database.Cursor;
import android.os.Bundle;
import android.view.View;
import android.widget.Button;
import android.widget.EditText;
import android.widget.Toast;

public class NoteEdit extends Activity {

    private EditText mTitleText;
    private EditText mBodyText;
    private Long mRowId;
    private NotesDbAdapter mDbHelper;

    @Override
    protected void onCreate(Bundle savedInstanceState) {
        super.onCreate(savedInstanceState);
        mDbHelper = new NotesDbAdapter(this);
        mDbHelper.open();

        setContentView(R.layout.note_edit);
        setTitle("Edit Note");

        mTitleText = (EditText) findViewById(R.id.title);
        mBodyText = (EditText) findViewById(R.id.body);

        Button confirmButton = (Button) findViewById(R.id.save);

        mRowId = (savedInstanceState == null) ? null :
                (Long) savedInstanceState.getSerializable(NotesDbAdapter.KEY_ROWID);
        if (mRowId == null) {
            Bundle extras = getIntent().getExtras();
            mRowId = extras != null ? extras.getLong(NotesDbAdapter.KEY_ROWID)
                    : null;
        }

        populateFields();

        confirmButton.setOnClickListener(new View.OnClickListener() {

            public void onClick(View view) {
                setResult(RESULT_OK);
                finish();
            }

        });
    }

    private void populateFields() {
        if (mRowId != null) {
            Cursor note = mDbHelper.fetchNote(mRowId);
            startManagingCursor(note);
            mTitleText.setText(note.getString(
                    note.getColumnIndexOrThrow(NotesDbAdapter.KEY_TITLE)));
```

```java
            mBodyText.setText(note.getString(
                    note.getColumnIndexOrThrow(NotesDbAdapter.KEY_BODY)));
        }
    }

    @Override
    protected void onSaveInstanceState(Bundle outState) {
        super.onSaveInstanceState(outState);
        saveState();
        outState.putSerializable(NotesDbAdapter.KEY_ROWID, mRowId);
    }

    @Override
    protected void onPause() {
        super.onPause();
        saveState();
    }

    @Override
    protected void onResume() {
        super.onResume();
        populateFields();
    }

    private void saveState() {
        String title = mTitleText.getText().toString();
        String body = mBodyText.getText().toString();

        if (title.equals(null) || "".equals(title) || body.equals(null) ||
"".equals(body)) {
            Toast.makeText(this, "No Data to be Save!", Toast.LENGTH_SHORT).show();
        } else {
            if (mRowId == null) {
                long id = mDbHelper.createNote(title, body);
                if (id > 0) {
                    mRowId = id;
                }
            } else {
                mDbHelper.updateNote(mRowId, title, body);
            }
        }
    }
}
```

Notepad

This is based on the Notepad.java class, this class will ensure all data from the database is shown as a list, allowing user to move from this Activity to the next with it extra data as to what the user selected or if user chose to delete a row.

```java
package com.alkathirikhalid.notepadapp;

import android.app.ListActivity;
import android.content.Intent;
import android.database.Cursor;
import android.os.Bundle;
import android.view.ContextMenu;
import android.view.Menu;
import android.view.MenuItem;
import android.view.View;
import android.widget.AdapterView;
import android.widget.ListView;
import android.widget.SimpleCursorAdapter;

public class Notepad extends ListActivity {
    private static final int ACTIVITY_CREATE = 0;
    private static final int ACTIVITY_EDIT = 1;

    private static final int INSERT_ID = Menu.FIRST;
    private static final int DELETE_ID = Menu.FIRST + 1;

    private NotesDbAdapter mDbHelper;

    /**
     * Called when the activity is first created.
     */
    @Override
    public void onCreate(Bundle savedInstanceState) {
        super.onCreate(savedInstanceState);
        setContentView(R.layout.notes_list);
        mDbHelper = new NotesDbAdapter(this);
        mDbHelper.open();
        fillData();
        registerForContextMenu(getListView());
    }

    private void fillData() {
        Cursor notesCursor = mDbHelper.fetchAllNotes();
        startManagingCursor(notesCursor);

        // Create an array to specify the fields we want to display in the list (only
TITLE)
        String[] from = new String[]{NotesDbAdapter.KEY_TITLE};

        // and an array of the fields we want to bind those fields to (in this case
just text1)
        int[] to = new int[]{R.id.text};

        // Now create a simple cursor adapter and set it to display
        SimpleCursorAdapter notes =
                new SimpleCursorAdapter(this, R.layout.notes_row, notesCursor, from,
to);
        setListAdapter(notes);
    }

    @Override
```

```java
public boolean onCreateOptionsMenu(Menu menu) {
    super.onCreateOptionsMenu(menu);
    menu.add(0, INSERT_ID, 0, "Add Note");
    return true;
}


@Override
public boolean onMenuItemSelected(int featureId, MenuItem item) {
    switch (item.getItemId()) {
        case INSERT_ID:
            createNote();
            return true;
    }

    return super.onMenuItemSelected(featureId, item);
}


@Override
public void onCreateContextMenu(ContextMenu menu, View v,
                                ContextMenu.ContextMenuInfo menuInfo) {
    super.onCreateContextMenu(menu, v, menuInfo);
    menu.add(0, DELETE_ID, 0, "Delete note");
}


@Override
public boolean onContextItemSelected(MenuItem item) {
    switch (item.getItemId()) {
        case DELETE_ID:
            AdapterView.AdapterContextMenuInfo info =
(AdapterView.AdapterContextMenuInfo) item.getMenuInfo();
            mDbHelper.deleteNote(info.id);
            fillData();
            return true;
    }
    return super.onContextItemSelected(item);
}

private void createNote() {
    Intent i = new Intent(this, NoteEdit.class);
    startActivityForResult(i, ACTIVITY_CREATE);
}

@Override
protected void onListItemClick(ListView l, View v, int position, long id) {
    super.onListItemClick(l, v, position, id);
    Intent i = new Intent(this, NoteEdit.class);
    i.putExtra(NotesDbAdapter.KEY_ROWID, id);
    startActivityForResult(i, ACTIVITY_EDIT);
}

@Override
protected void onActivityResult(int requestCode, int resultCode, Intent intent) {
    super.onActivityResult(requestCode, resultCode, intent);
    fillData();
}
}
```

Manifest

Based on the AndroidManifest.xml file, this fill will show all our Activity classes and which one is the Entry point to the Application as specified by Action Main and Category Launcher.

```xml
<?xml version="1.0" encoding="utf-8"?>
<manifest xmlns:android="http://schemas.android.com/apk/res/android"
    package="com.alkathirikhalid.notepadapp">

    <application
        android:allowBackup="true"
        android:icon="@mipmap/ic_launcher"
        android:label="@string/app_name"
        android:supportsRtl="true"
        android:theme="@style/AppTheme">
        <activity android:name=".Notepad">
            <intent-filter>
                <action android:name="android.intent.action.MAIN" />

                <category android:name="android.intent.category.LAUNCHER" />
            </intent-filter>
        </activity>
        <activity android:name=".NoteEdit" />
    </application>

</manifest>
```

Fig. 4.16 | Empty List

Add Note

Fig. 4.17 | Add Note

Fig. 4.18 | Adding Title and Body

Knowledge Check

1. Explain what does this code do in xml '@+id/...'
2. What does the below code do?
   a. android:layout_width="match_parent"
   b. android:layout_height="wrap_content"
3. You want the view objects to be aligned from top to bottom in a LinearLayout how would you achieve this?
4. How can we access a view object in xml into our java code?
5. Explain hardcoded string and how to avoid them
6. What happens in the Notepad example provided above during onPause() and onResume()?
7. How Many Activities dose Notepad App have?
8. Name the launcher Activity Class in Notepad
9. What do you need in order to iterate through values in the database as shown in the Notepad application Example?
10. What does the finish() method do in Notepad application sample

Lab Exercise

1. Build the Notepad App and run as provided in the code
2. (Optional) Do any improvements that are useful and can be done to the UI or Backend code to improve the Notepad App.

Chapter 5

Introduction

As we have seen in the previous chapters on how to setup, code and which place to code, arrange and organize our code in Android, here we will design, build and run our application following the procedures we have introduced in the previous chapters.

Audio Recorder

We are going to build an app that records audio and stores it in the user device, this app is going to a one button app that take the user from step to step by changing the button and functionality of that button from:

- Record (beginning)
- Stop (Active while recording)
- Play (Active after stopping audio recording)
- Stop (Active while playing)
- Record (End)

Audio Recorder Design

As we have seen the flow from Beginning to the End the UI design for our Audio Recorder App will be simple using the Figures as for:

- Record Fig. 5.1.
- Stop Fig. 5.2.
- Play Fig. 5.3.

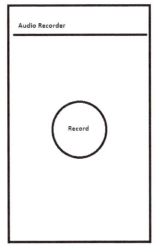

Fig. 5.1 | Record UI

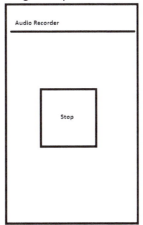

Fig 5.2 | Stop UI

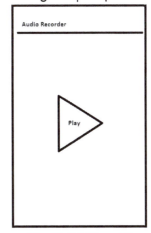

Fig. 5.3 | Play UI

Audio Recorder Build

Let's get started Start a new Android Studio Project Fig. 5.4. and call it Audio Recorder Fig. 5.5.

- Application name: Audio Recorder
- Company Domain: alkathirikhalid.com
- Package name: default
- Project location: default

For the company domain you may use the above for building locally or any that you own, except for example.com which Play Store won't accept, and on top of that if you name your package to a domain other than the one's your own it will bring problems as Play Store uniquely identifies an app based on its package name, so it must be unique.

#TIP 21: When uploading to play store, use a domain name that you own example org.x or com.x etc. when uploading an app use something like org.x.appname or com.x.appname then the package naming must be unique for each different app and must be the same for the same up while or when updating the up or upgrading.

— ✕

Android Studio
Version 2.1.2

⚙ Start a new Android Studio project

📁 Open an existing Android Studio project

⬇ Check out project from Version Control ▾

📝 Import project (Eclipse ADT, Gradle, etc.)

📋 Import an Android code sample

⚙ Configure ▾   Get Help ▾

Fig. 5.4 | Start a new Android Studio project

Fig. 5.5 | Configure your new project

Now we need to set the Target Android Devices, we could head and select multiple platforms but here we are coding exclusively for Android Mobile devices so select Phone and Tablet, go ahead and select the Minimum SDK:

- API 16: Android 4.1 Jelly Bean Fig. 5.6.

This should cover around 95.2% of the total devices connecting to Play Store at the moment this application was being created, the value will change with time, as previously explained while creating First App.

Once you have selected the API level click Next.

Next Add an Activity for our App, we go ahead and select an Empty Activity as we will need to construct everything from scratch. Fig. 5.7.

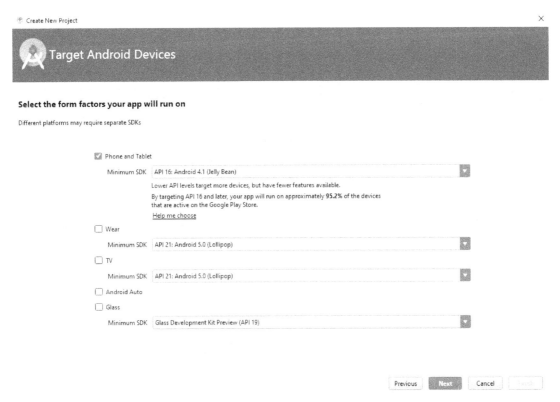

Fig. 5.6 | Target Android Devices

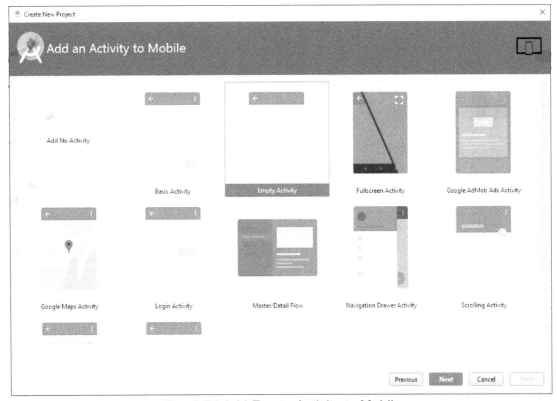

Fig. 5.7 | Add Empty Activity to Mobile

Now we need to customize our Activity by giving it a name and whether we want to create and XML layout for it or not Fig. 5.8. For this Application leave everything default. Android Studio will create the two files for us automatic:

- MainActivity.java
- Activity_main.xml

At the same time the created files will have a predefined generate default code for us which we can either remove, replace or simply use it the way it is as shown in Fig. 5.9.

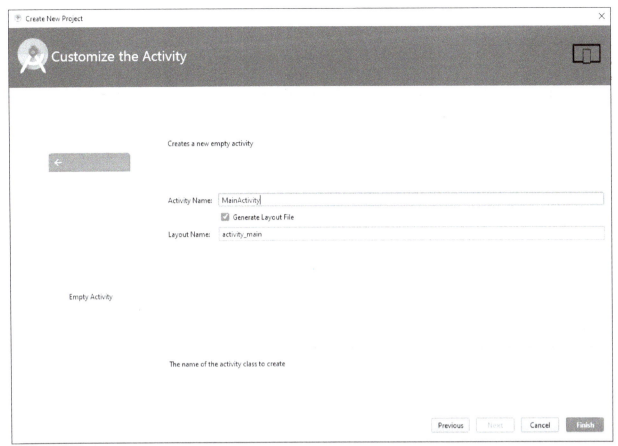

Fig. 5.8 | Customize the Activity

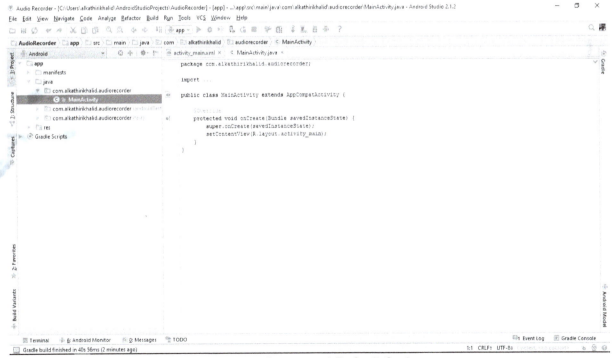

Fig. 5.9 | Generated Default Code

Our Skeletal Application is created Fig. 5.10. and can be deployed to a mobile device or AVD for testing, this should give you the "Hello World!" output on your device.

We are going to modify the look and feel of the application, there are a lot of setting that can be achieved from the AndroidManifest file one of them being android theme, we can enforce a specific theme for the whole application with in the application tag as seen in Fig. 5.11.

(Optional) Go ahead and include the line within your manifest file to force the theme to be Light, remember since we are using support libraries we will need to specify the theme from AppCompat library

- `android:theme="@style/Base.Theme.AppCompat.Light"`

Rather than

- `android:theme="@android:style/Theme.Holo.Light"`

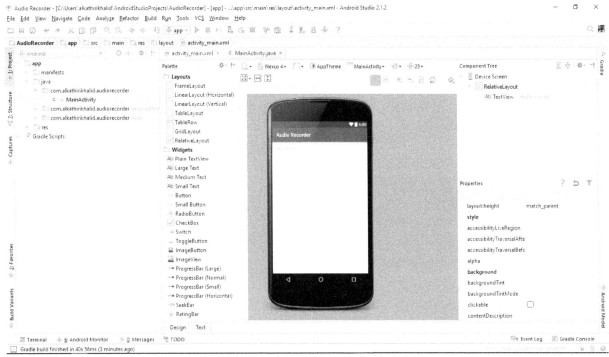

Fig. 5.10 | Skeletal Application

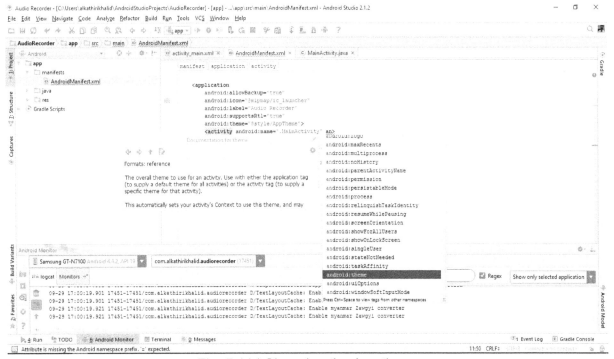

Fig. 5.11 | Changing the App theme

We can also go ahead and enable version control Fig. 5.12. to keep track of our application development and progress this is important to keep track of your application as explained in previous chapters.

- VCS > Enable Version Control Integration

Then Select the version Control System, we specify Git. fig. 5.13.

Fig. 5.12 | Enable Version Control Integration

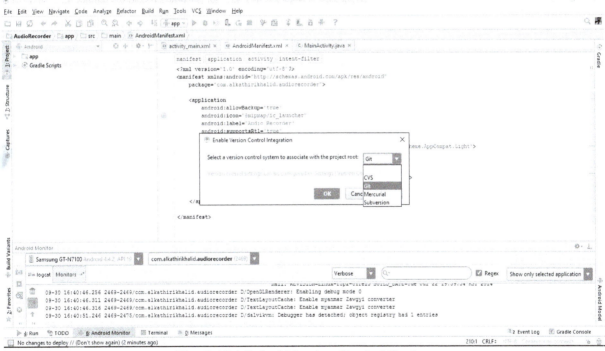

Fig. 5.13 | Select Version Control System

Front End Coding

Here we are going to code our app to reflect the look we have design previously, to achieve this we will need to do some modification to the code.

Change the layout

Android comes with multiple layouts namely:

- FrameLayout
- LinearLayout (Horizontal)
- LinearLayout (Vertical)
- TableLayout
- TableRow
- GridLayout
- RelativeLayout

Our app is by default constructed with RelativeLayout whereby the view objects are relative to each other or the screen such as being dragged and drop on the position relative to other objects on screen, we will convert this to LinearLayout (Vertical) Fig.5.14. so that the view objects are on top of each other to bring about balance and symmetry we will also center our view objects using gravity.

Original Code

```xml
<?xml version="1.0" encoding="utf-8"?>
<RelativeLayout xmlns:android="http://schemas.android.com/apk/res/android"
    xmlns:tools="http://schemas.android.com/tools"
    android:layout_width="match_parent"
    android:layout_height="match_parent"
    android:paddingBottom="@dimen/activity_vertical_margin"
    android:paddingLeft="@dimen/activity_horizontal_margin"
    android:paddingRight="@dimen/activity_horizontal_margin"
    android:paddingTop="@dimen/activity_vertical_margin"
    tools:context="com.alkathirikhalid.audiorecorder.MainActivity">

    <TextView
        android:layout_width="wrap_content"
        android:layout_height="wrap_content"
        android:text="Hello World!" />
</RelativeLayout>
```

Based on our design we have a button and we will add a text in the bottom to allow user to play previous recorded audio if any. Press Ctrl+Alt+L to format the code. Our app should launch with default functionalities and that is to record, for that we will set our default image to a record image and text to Record. As seen in fig. 5.15.

We could use in built android images but this might lead to problems in the event Android stops support for such resource example:

- `android:background="@android:drawable/ic_media_play"`

Fig. 5.14 | Selecting Linearlayout

Fig. 5.15 | Creating record image from Clipart

So the best solution is to either create the images directly on Android Studio or saving them ourselves in the drawable directory, that way Android will use your resources from your app that will always be installed together rather than using Android resources which some of the themes might be deprecated and removed in future. I found the created record image ugly hence included one that is red as seen in Fig. 5.16.

Modified Code

```
<?xml version="1.0" encoding="utf-8"?>
<LinearLayout xmlns:android="http://schemas.android.com/apk/res/android"
    xmlns:tools="http://schemas.android.com/tools"
    android:layout_width="match_parent"
    android:layout_height="match_parent"
    android:gravity="center"
    android:orientation="vertical"
    android:paddingBottom="@dimen/activity_vertical_margin"
    android:paddingLeft="@dimen/activity_horizontal_margin"
    android:paddingRight="@dimen/activity_horizontal_margin"
    android:paddingTop="@dimen/activity_vertical_margin"
    tools:context="com.alkathirikhalid.audiorecorder.MainActivity">

    <Button
        android:id="@+id/button"
        android:layout_width="wrap_content"
        android:layout_height="wrap_content"
        android:background="@drawable/ic_audio_record_red"
        android:text="@string/record" />
</LinearLayout>
```

The changes done to the UI that we have covered so far are:
- Changing the UI Theme in the Manifest
- Changing the Layout from RelativeLayout to LinearLayout
- Setting the Orientation to Vertical
- Setting Gravity to Center
- Removing the TextView
- Adding a Button
- Setting a Button Background
- Setting a Button Text
- Adding the text String as a Resource

TIP #22: Ensure everything needed in app/src/main/* is added to your source control in this case to git and all the stages changes are committed. Fig. 5.17.

Fig. 5.16 | Audio Recorder Default launch view

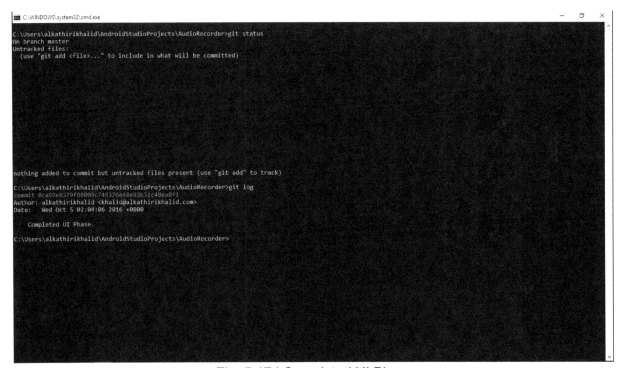

Fig. 5.17 | Completed UI Phase

Back End Coding

Here we are going to code on our Audio recorder to perform task such as Record, Stop and Play in that order.

Setting a Button

We have added a button in the Layout which by default it appears as a Record button, we now need to make Android aware of this object being a button by declaring, initializing and assigning it a name Fig. 5.18, before making the button dynamic and responsive to user interaction, we achieve that by:

```java
import android.widget.Button;
...
/**
* Button to record, stop and play audio
*/
private Button button;
...
//Find View Objects/Button by its ID
button = (Button) findViewById(R.id.button);
```

Now our button object (Layout ID) is linked to button object (java code) by using the findViewById method, this method is used to find all view objects from a layout.

We need to intercept user clicks performed on this particular object, we achieve that by using an onClickListener Fig. 5.19, we can either declare it or implement one into our Activity, the best recommended way is to implement one as creating new Objects takes a load on the memory if we were to deal with multiple buttons or other objects, we achieve this by:

```java
import android.view.View.OnClickListener;
...
public class MainActivity extends AppCompatActivity implements OnClickListener {
...
/**
* Implemented method only either Record, Play or Stop isActive.
* Based on the set flag
*/
@Override
public void onClick(View v) {

    }
}
```

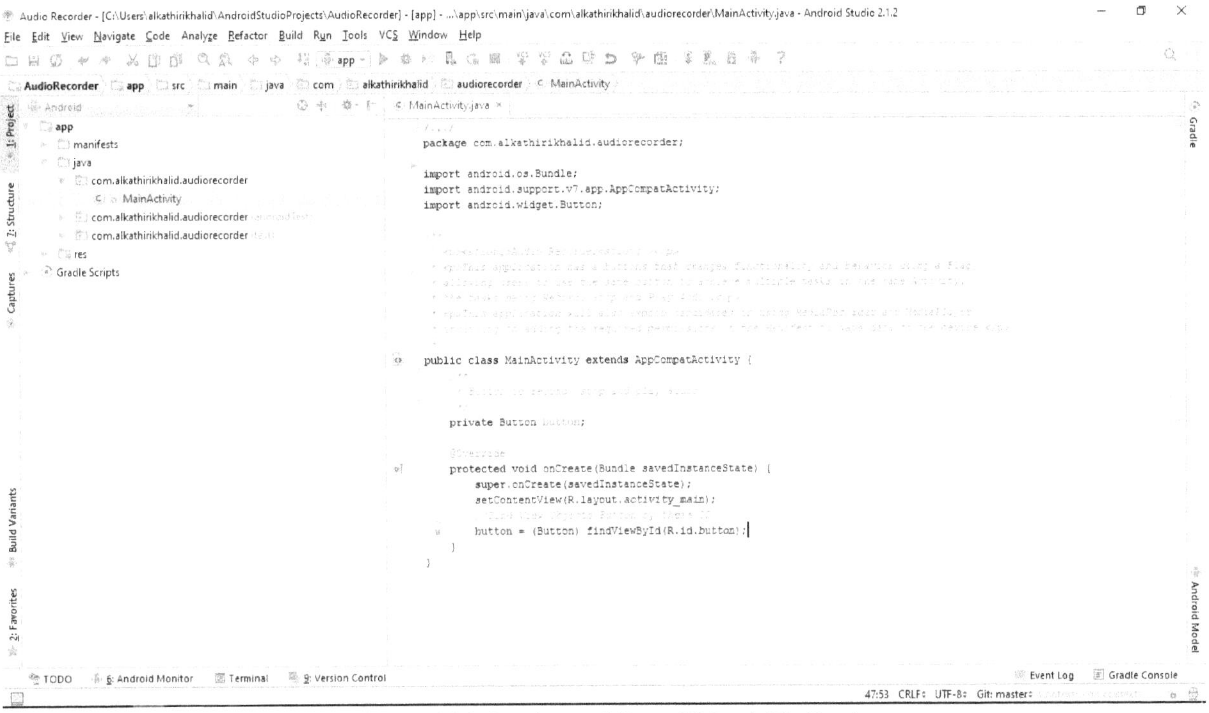

Fig. 5.18 | Setting a View Object (Button)

Fig. 5.19 | Implementing OnClickListener

After all that we now binding our OnClickListener to our object which is our primary button by using the method setOnClickListener right after below findViewByID method, since we implemented the onClickListener we simply use 'this' to specify the onClickListener Fig. 5.20.

```
...
// Bind the OnClickLister to button
button.setOnClickListener(this);
...
```

Setting File Path

We need to set the storage location for our audio file, we will declare a simple static string to achieve this or you can you path whichever you are more comfortable with.

```
/**
 * Audio file storage location name
 */
private static String fileName;
```

We now need to find the device storage path, as we now know Android runs on a multitude of devices and each device manufacturer is free and independent on the hardware and hardware setting they have for their device, this bring a problem unlike in windows you can start a path directly from C: but in Android they have different name depending on what the manufacture, to be on the safe side we will let Android OS running on the device give us a path name Fig. 5.21.

```
import android.os.Environment;
...
// Sets the file location name using Android OS Environment
fileName = Environment.getExternalStorageDirectory().getAbsolutePath() +
"/audiorecorder.3gp";
...
```

Checking if External Storage is Available.

```
// Checks if external storage is available for read and write
public boolean isExternalStorageWritable() {
    String state = Environment.getExternalStorageState();
    if (Environment.MEDIA_MOUNTED.equals(state)) {
        return true;
    }
    return false;
}

// Checks if external storage is available to at least read
public boolean isExternalStorageReadable() {
    String state = Environment.getExternalStorageState();
    if (Environment.MEDIA_MOUNTED.equals(state) ||
            Environment.MEDIA_MOUNTED_READ_ONLY.equals(state)) {
        return true;
    }
    return false;
}
```

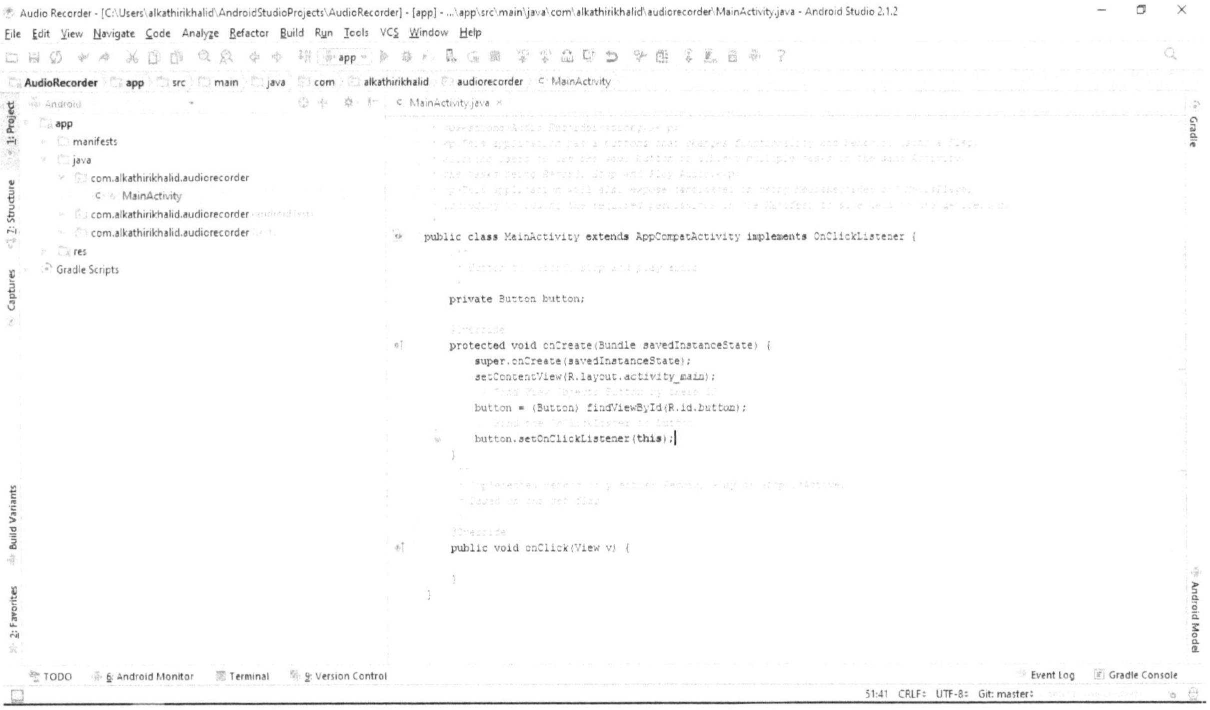

Fig. 5.20 | Binding OnClickListener to button

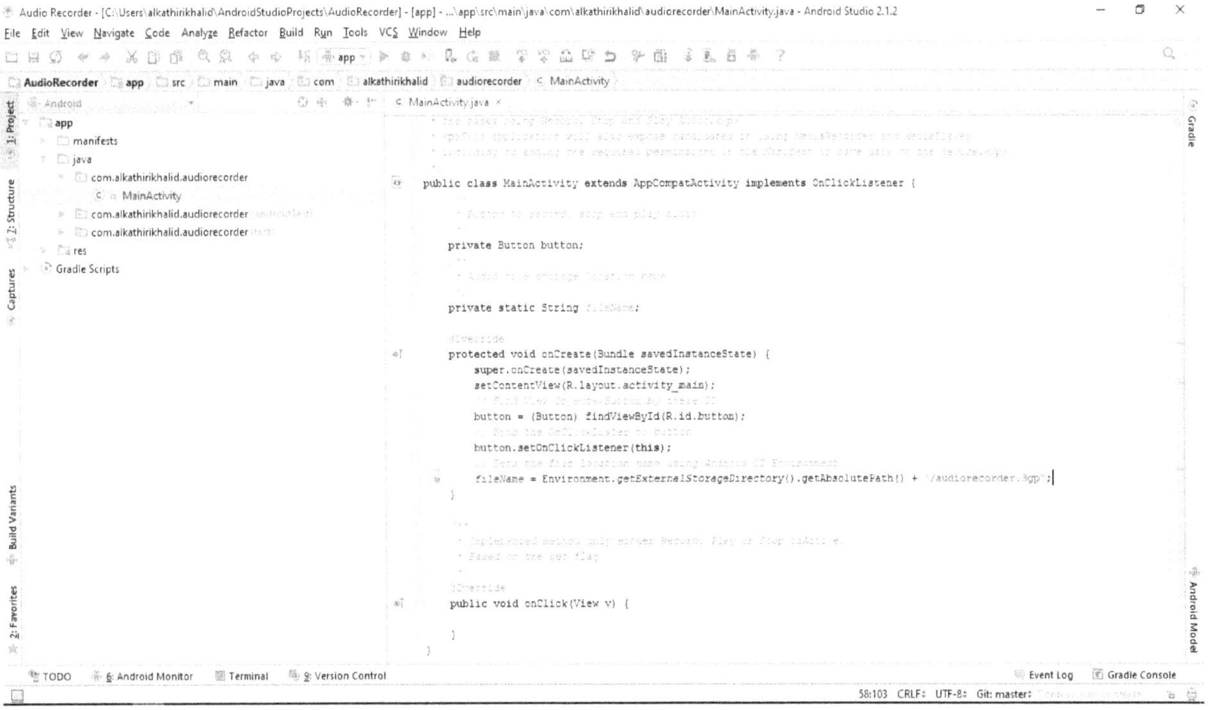

Fig. 5.21 | Storage Directory from Android Environment

Setting MediaRecorder and MediaPlayer

As the name suggest MediaRecorder is for recording and MediaPlayer is for playing audio files, we declare them in our Activity.

```
...
/**
 * MediaRecorder Obj for recording
 */
private MediaRecorder mediaRecorder;
/**
 * MediaPlayer Obj for playing
 */
private MediaPlayer mediaPlayer;
...
```

We also need to be notified once the playing is completed, for this we need a listener and Android has a specific lister known as onCompletionListener which will notify as once play is completed, we are going to implement this into our Activity Fig. 5.22.

```
...
import android.media.MediaPlayer.OnCompletionListener;
...
public class MainActivity extends AppCompatActivity implements OnClickListener,
OnCompletionListener {
...
/**
 * Listening on Play Completion
 *
 * @param mediaPlayer
 */
@Override
public void onCompletion(MediaPlayer mediaPlayer) {

    }
...
}
```

Fig. 5.22 | Adding OnCompletionListener

We have mediaPlayer and MediaRecord but we are not using them yet, we will add them to specific methods to be triggered and used based on the user clicks on our button, the methods being:

- startRecording()
- stopRecording()
- startPlaying()
- stopPlaying()

```
...
/**
 * Start Recording
 */
private void startRecording() {

}

/**
 * Stop Recording
 */
private void stopRecording() {

}

/**
 * Start Playing
 */
private void startPlaying() {

}

/**
 * Stop Playing
 */
private void stopPlaying() {

}
...
```

TIP #23: Remember to add your source code to git for every progressive change you make, the easiest way to achieve this in Android Studio is by clicking Ctrl+alt+A Fig. 5.23.

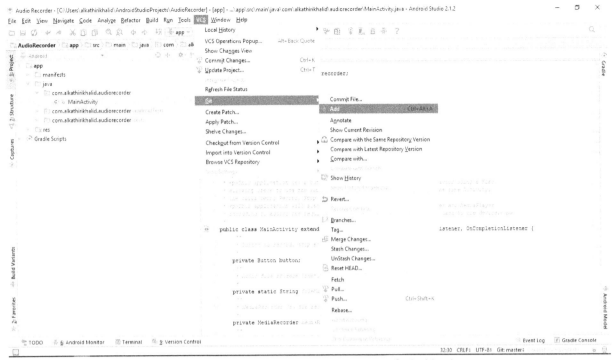

Fig. 5.23 | Add to Git using shortcut Ctrl+Alt+A

We now have empty methods that can be used for our Application appropriately we will start with startRecording method.

```java
...
/**
 * Start Recording
 */
private void startRecording() {
    // Instantiate a new MediaRecorder Obj named mediaRecorder
    mediaRecorder = new MediaRecorder();
    // Set Audio Source from Microphone
    mediaRecorder.setAudioSource(MediaRecorder.AudioSource.MIC);
    // Set audio format as .3gp
    mediaRecorder.setOutputFormat(MediaRecorder.OutputFormat.THREE_GPP);
    // Set audio file location to be saved
    mediaRecorder.setOutputFile(fileName);
    // Set audio encoder to AMR for backward compatibility
    mediaRecorder.setAudioEncoder(MediaRecorder.AudioEncoder.AMR_NB);
    // Initialize mediaRecorder to start and catch the IOException
    try {
        mediaRecorder.prepare();
    } catch (IOException e) {
        e.printStackTrace();
    }
    // Start Recording
    mediaRecorder.start();
}
...
```

Let's fill up, stopRecording, It is good practice to call release method when you're done using the MediaRecorder. whenever an Activity of an application is paused its onPause() method is called, or stopped its onStop() method is called, this method should be invoked to release the MediaRecorder object, unless the application has a special need to keep the object around. In addition to unnecessary resources example memory and instances of codecs being held, failure to call this method immediately if a MediaRecorder object is no longer needed may also lead to continuous battery consumption for mobile devices, and recording failure for other applications if no multiple instances of the same codec are supported on a device Fig. 5.24.

```java
...
private void stopRecording() {
    // Release the Obj resources
    mediaRecorder.release();
}
...
```

```
private void startRecording() {
    mediaRecorder = new MediaRecorder();
    mediaRecorder.setAudioSource(MediaRecorder.AudioSource.MIC);
    mediaRecorder.setOutputFormat(MediaRecorder.OutputFormat.THREE_GPP);
    mediaRecorder.setOutputFile(fileName);
    mediaRecorder.setAudioEncoder(MediaRecorder.AudioEncoder.AMR_NB);
    try {
        mediaRecorder.prepare();
    } catch (IOException e) {
        e.printStackTrace();
    }
    mediaRecorder.start();
}

private void stopRecording() {
    mediaRecorder.release();
}
```

Fig. 5.24. startRecording() and stopRecording()

We will tackle startPlaying() method is somewhat similar to startRecording()

```java
...
/**
 * Start Playing
 */
private void startPlaying() {
    // Instantiate a new MediaPlayer Obj named mediaPlayer
    mediaPlayer = new MediaPlayer();
    // Bind the onCompletionListener to mediaPlayer to be notified of successful
playback
    mediaPlayer.setOnCompletionListener(this);
    // Set audio data source and catch the IOException
    try {
        mediaPlayer.setDataSource(fileName);
    } catch (IOException e) {
        e.printStackTrace();
    }
    // Initialize mediaPlayer to start and catch the IOException
    try {
        mediaPlayer.prepare();
    } catch (IOException e) {
        e.printStackTrace();
    }
    // Start Playing
    mediaPlayer.start();
}
...
```

Let's fill up, stopPlaying(), it is also somewhat similar to StopRecording().

```java
...
/**
 * Stop Playing
 */
private void stopPlaying() {
    // Release the Obj resources
    mediaPlayer.release();
}
...
```

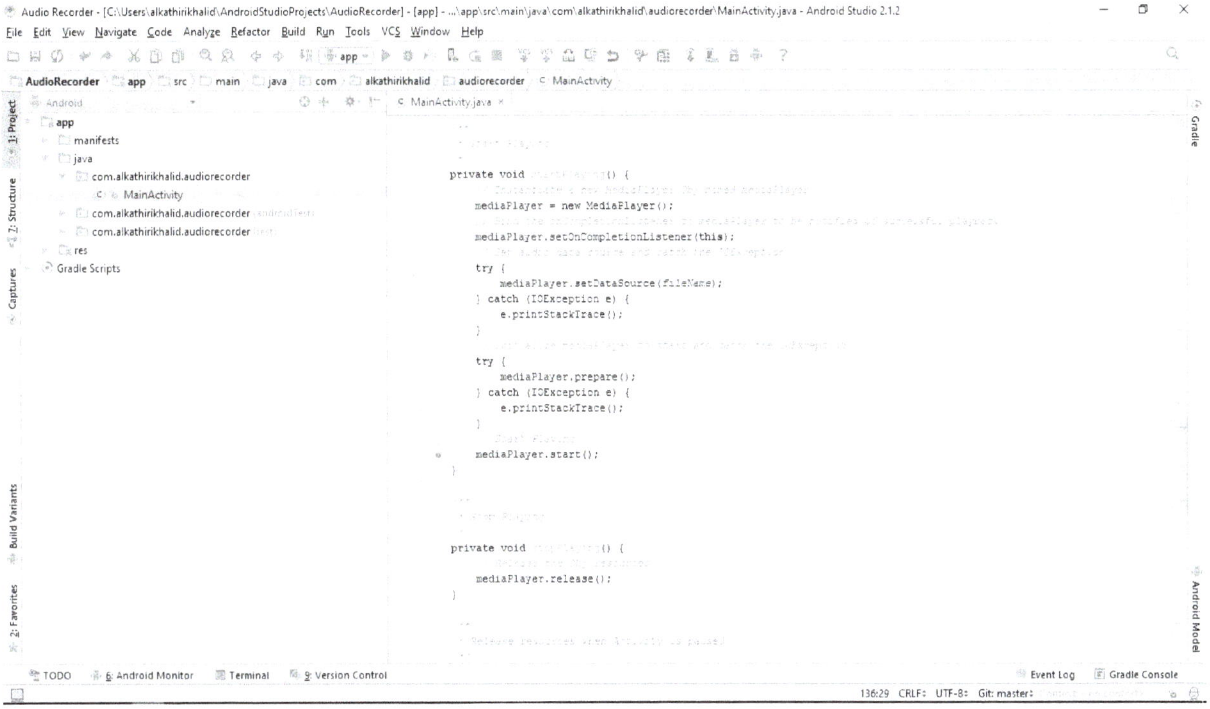

Fig. 5.25. startPlaying() and stopPlaying()

Setting Activity Flow

We also need to handle when the Activity is onPause() and onStop() as we need to release the resources.

```java
...
/**
 * Release resources when Activity is paused
 */
@Override
protected void onPause() {
    super.onPause();
    // Release the mediaRecorder resources
    if (mediaRecorder != null) {
        mediaRecorder.release();
    }
    // Release the mediaPlayer resources
    if (mediaPlayer != null) {
        mediaPlayer.release();
    }
}

/**
 * Release resources when Activity is stopped
 */
@Override
protected void onStop() {
    super.onStop();
    // Release the mediaRecorder resources
    if (mediaRecorder != null) {
        mediaRecorder.release();
    }
    // Release the mediaPlayer resources
    if (mediaPlayer != null) {
        mediaPlayer.release();
    }
}
...
```

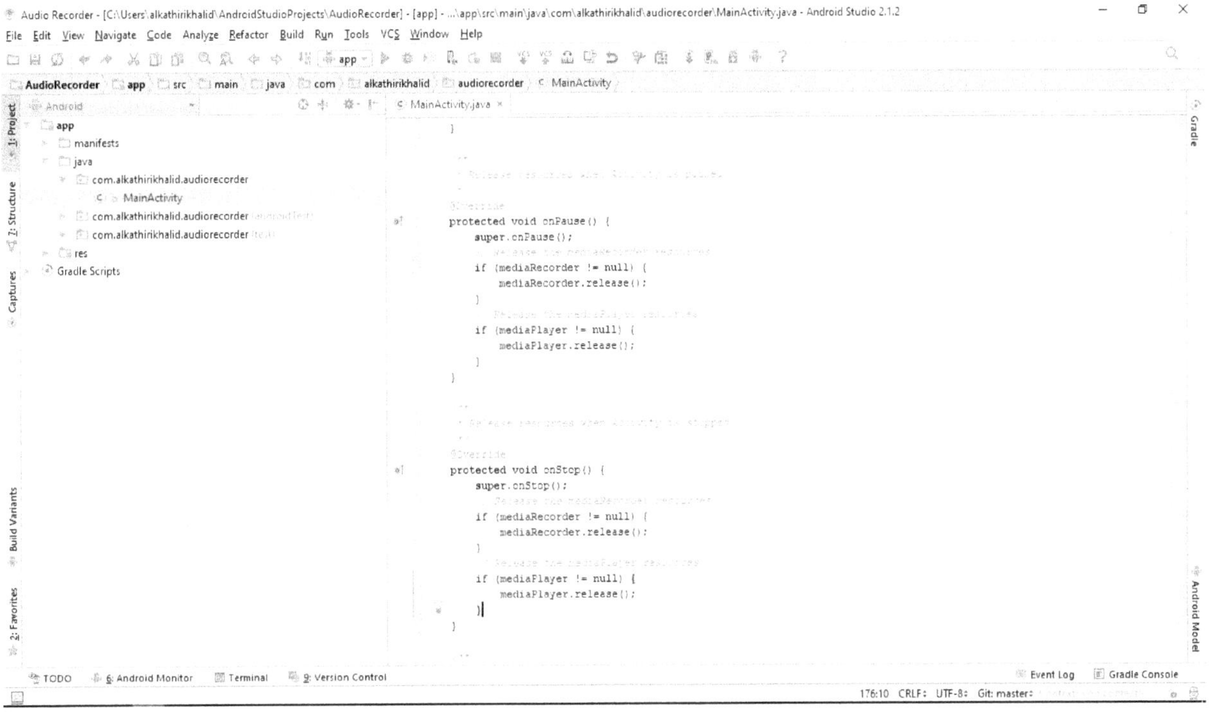

Fig. 5.26. onPause() and onStop()

Setting AudioRecorder Logic

Since we only have one button and need to make it dynamic to sustain all the steps a user may take with that one button from Start Recording, Stop Recording, Start Playing and Stop Playing, to achieve this we add a Boolean Flag in our Activity and set it too True on isRecoding the first time a user starts the App within the onCreate method, meaning immediately the app is up and running then the first step is to allow user to record, the rest we will set to false Fig. 5.27.

```java
...
/**
 * Toggle button function by using flags isStartRecording,
 * isStopRecording, isStartPlaying and isStopPlaying
 */
private boolean isStartRecording, isStopRecording, isStartPlaying, isStopPlaying;
...
// Allow user to start Recording
isStartRecording = Boolean.TRUE;
// Disable stop recording, start playing and stop playing
isStopRecording = isStartPlaying = isStopPlaying = Boolean.FALSE;
...
```

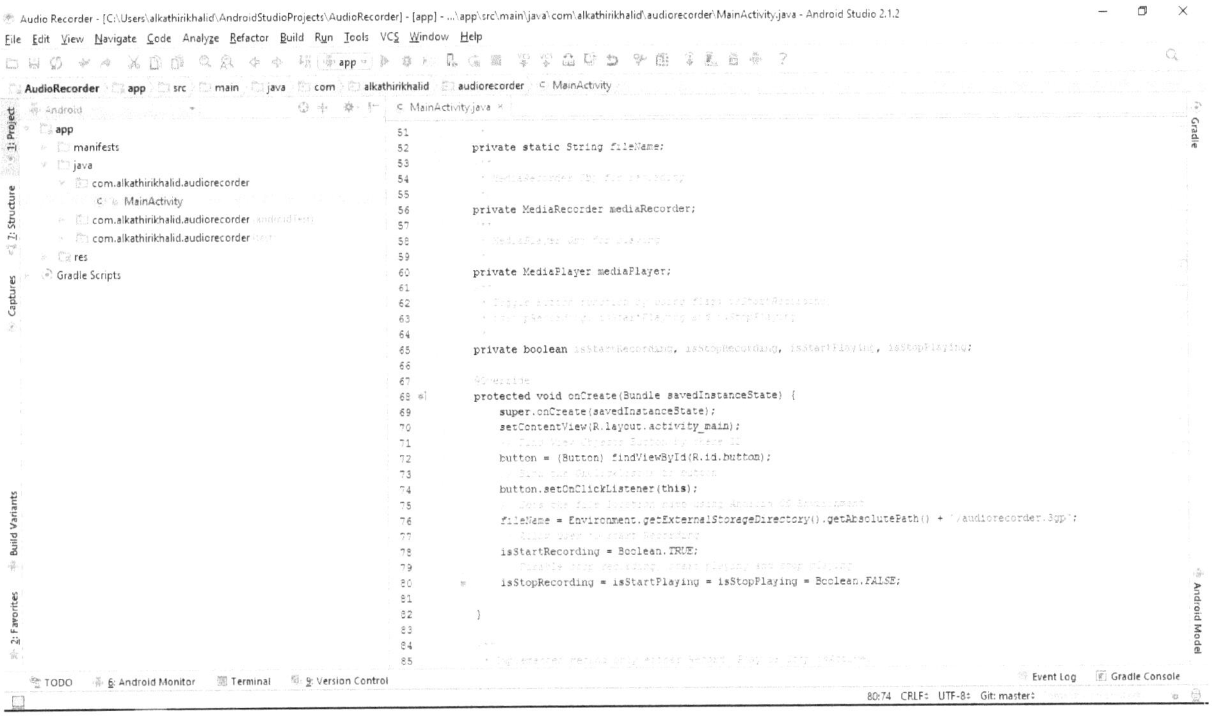

Fig. 5.27 | Audio Recorder Logic

Setting Permission to Record Audio

We will need the user to grant Audio Recording permission to our application so it can record Audio using the device microphone and permission to write to storage, for this we will need to permission in the Androidmanifest file.

Click on manifest folder and select AndroidManifest and add as seen in Fig. 5.28:

```
...
<!-- Permission to Record Audio from Microphone -->
<uses-permission android:name="android.permission.RECORD_AUDIO" />
<!-- Permission to read and write to and from storage -->
<uses-permission android:name="android.permission.WRITE_EXTERNAL_STORAGE" />
...
```

Fig. 5.28 | Adding Permission to AndroidManifest

Our Application is almost complete, we need to generate the resources both images and string resource for the remaining button mutation to Stop Recording, Start Playing, Stop Playing and change the launcher image. So far we only have one which is Start Recording the red image with our string resource.

Changing Launcher Icon

New > Image Asset > IC_Launcher Fig. 5.29.
And Override the existing default image with the newly created one Fig. 5.30.

We will select the microphone which closely resembles the purpose of our application and that is to Record Audio.

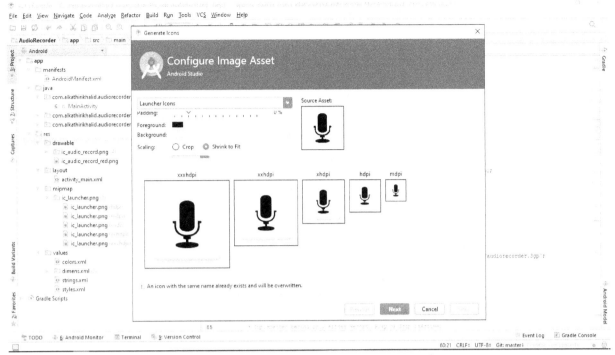

Fig. 5.29 | Image Asset of Type Launcher Icon

Fig. 5.30 | Override existing Image Launcher

Using the same procedure as previously explained, generate the rest of the image resources for Stop Recording, Start Playing and Stop Playing. Making all recording red and all playing blue Fig. 5.31.

You may choose to generate proper images or download a few from free stock online that would make the application not functional only but more appealing in nature.

We also need to set the String resources for the image text, within values add the following:

```xml
<resources>
    <string name="app_name">Audio Recorder</string>
    <string name="record">Record</string>
    <string name="stop_record">Stop Record</string>
    <string name="play">Play</string>
    <string name="stop_play">Stop Play</string>
</resources>
```

You have the option to edit for all other supported languages by clicking the link above Open Editor as seen in Fig. 5.32.

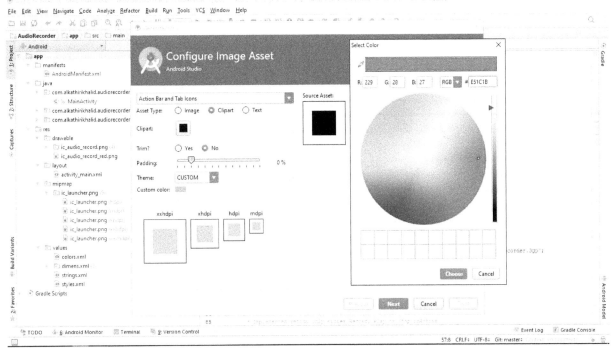

Fig. 5.31 | Creating Image Resources

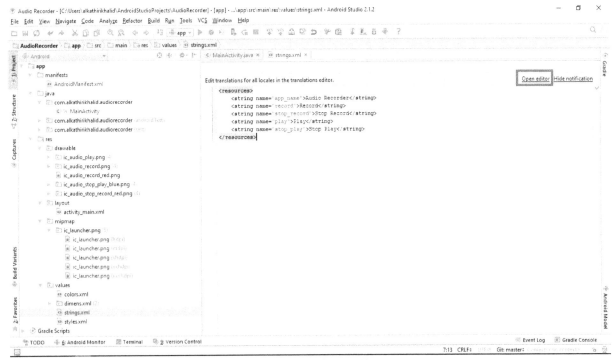

Fig. 5.32 | Creating String Resources

Make the Application work

Here we simply need to call any method that we desire and have a checking on which step a user is in. We will need to modify onClick method to include a checking whether our button is clicked by using a Switch, this is unnecessary as we only have one button and the click method is triggered if any view being binded triggered it, for good practice we will include it and also a second checking to see which Flag is active deactivate it and activate the second step.

```java
...
/**
 * Implemented method only either Record, Play or Stop isActive.
 * Based on the set flag
 */
@Override
public void onClick(View v) {
    switch (v.getId()) {
        // Only this button ID will be triggered
        case R.id.button:
            if (isStartRecording) {
                // Start Recording
                startRecording();
                // Deactivate Start Recording
                isStartRecording = !isStartRecording;
                // Activate Stop Recording
                isStopRecording = !isStopRecording;
                // Change button image
                button.setBackgroundResource(R.drawable.ic_audio_stop_record_red);
                // Change button text
                button.setText(R.string.stop_record);
            } else if (isStopRecording) {
                // Stop Recording
                stopRecording();
                // Deactivate Stop Recording
                isStopRecording = !isStopRecording;
                // Activate Start Playing
                isStartPlaying = !isStartPlaying;
                // Change button image
                button.setBackgroundResource(R.drawable.ic_audio_play);
                // Change button text
                button.setText(R.string.play);
            } else if (isStartPlaying) {
                // Start Playing
                startPlaying();
                // Deactivate Start Playing
                isStartPlaying = !isStartPlaying;
                // Activate stop Playing
                isStopPlaying = !isStopPlaying;
                // Change button image
                button.setBackgroundResource(R.drawable.ic_audio_stop_play_blue);
                // Change button text
                button.setText(R.string.stop_play);

            } else if (isStopPlaying) {
                // Stop Recording
                stopPlaying();
                // Deactivate Stop Recording
                isStopPlaying = !isStopPlaying;
                // Activate Start Recording
                isStartRecording = !isStopRecording;
                // Change button image
                button.setBackgroundResource(R.drawable.ic_audio_record_red);
                // Change button text
                button.setText(R.string.record);
```

```
        } else {
            // This line will never be executed added for best practice
            Toast.makeText(this, R.string.unknown_action,
Toast.LENGTH_SHORT).show();
        }
        break;
    default:
        // This line will never be executed added for best practice
        Toast.makeText(this, R.string.unknown_button_click,
Toast.LENGTH_SHORT).show();
        break;
    }
}
...
```

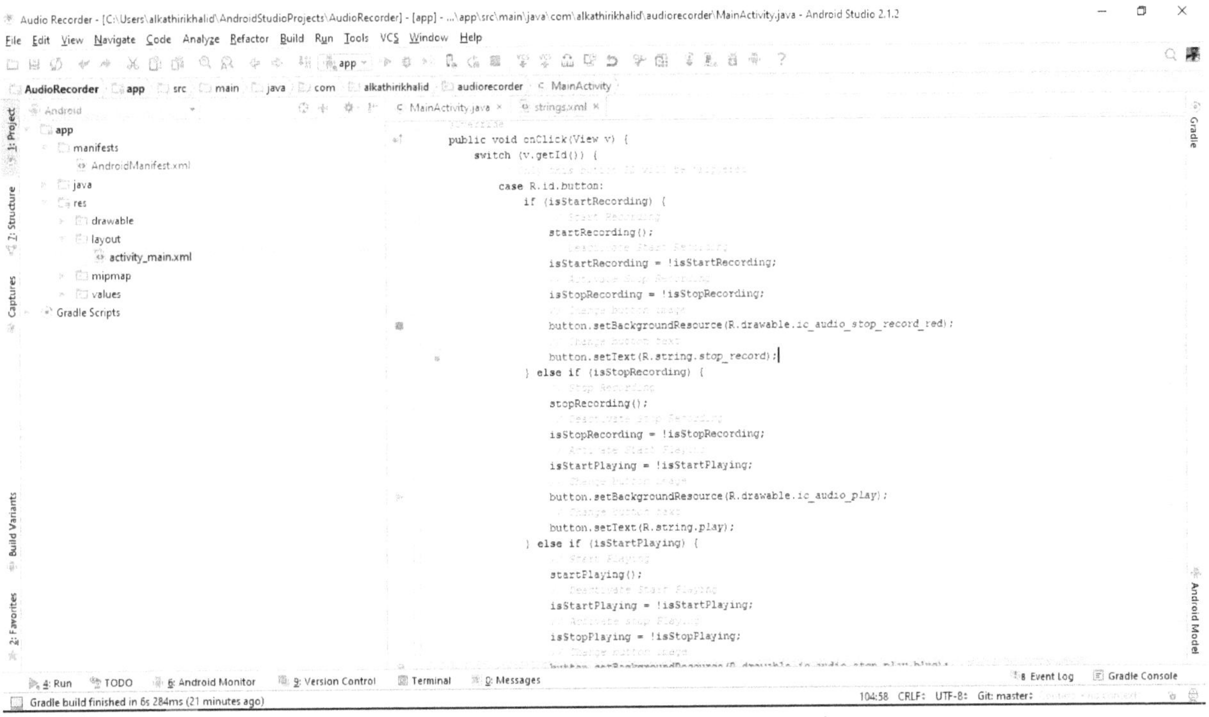

Fig. 5.33 | Modified onClick method

We will also need to modify the OnCompletion Method so as in the event a user does not click stop play the app automatically detects it has completed playing and it should do the same thing as what is expected when the use stops playing the recorded audio as seen in Fig 5.34.

```java
...
/**
 * Listening on Play Completion
 *
 * @param mediaPlayer
 */
@Override
public void onCompletion(MediaPlayer mediaPlayer) {
    // Stop Recording
    stopPlaying();
    // Deactivate Stop Recording
    isStopPlaying = !isStopPlaying;
    // Activate Start Recording
    isStartRecording = !isStopRecording;
    // Change button image
    button.setBackgroundResource(R.drawable.ic_audio_record_red);
    // Change button text
    button.setText(R.string.record);
}
...
```

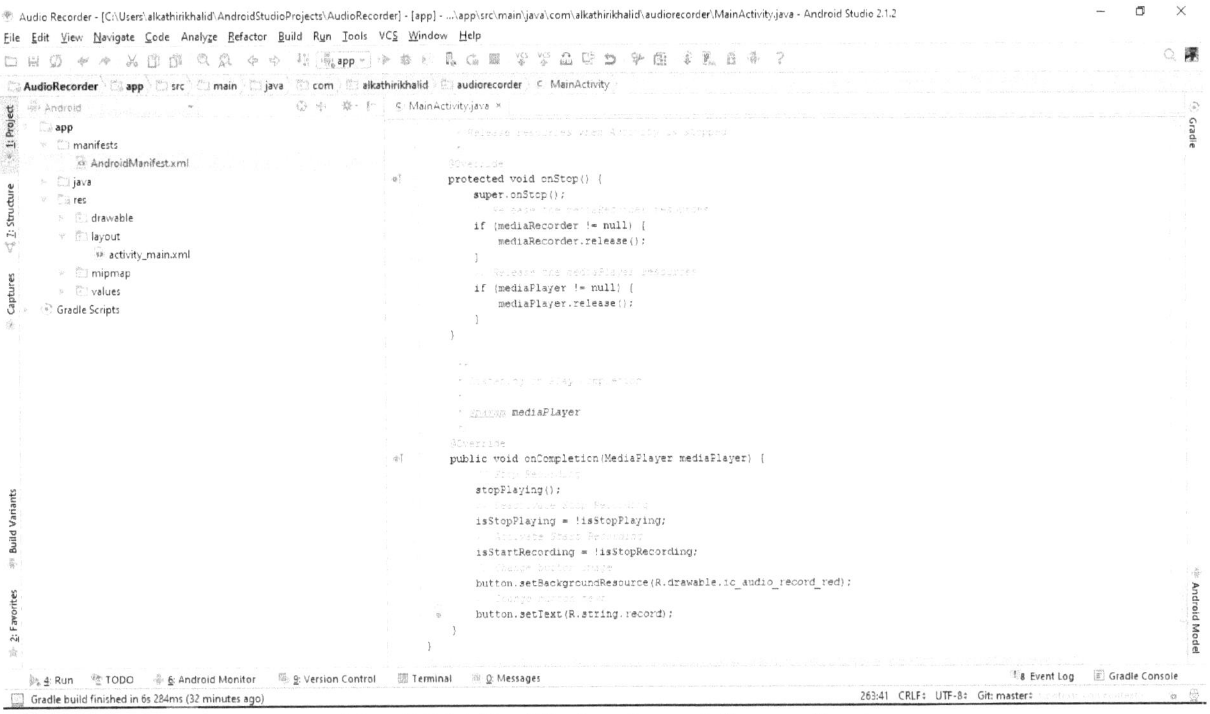

Fig. 5.34 | Modified onCompletion method

Launch Audio Record

Let's click Run or Shift+F10 to launch the app into your device or AVD, you will be prompted to pick a device to run this application, here we select a mobile device to install our app and test it Fig. 5.35.

The device we choose will be our deployment target, make sure the device meets the minimum Android requirement for our application and that is API 16. If this requirement is not met our application won't install and an error will be shown.

We can now see our launcher Icon in our devices, this icon is dynamic and android environment picks the best icon size to fit the device screen resolution see Fig. 5.36.

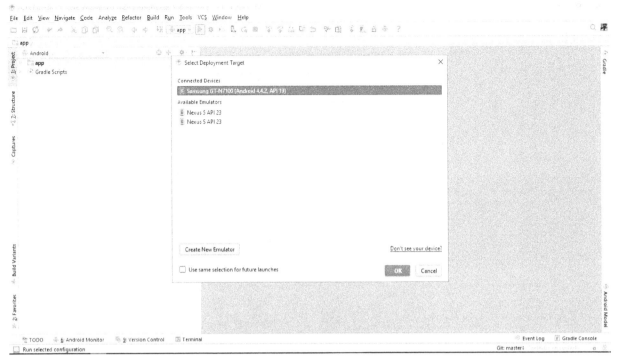

Fig. 5.35 | Select Deployment Target

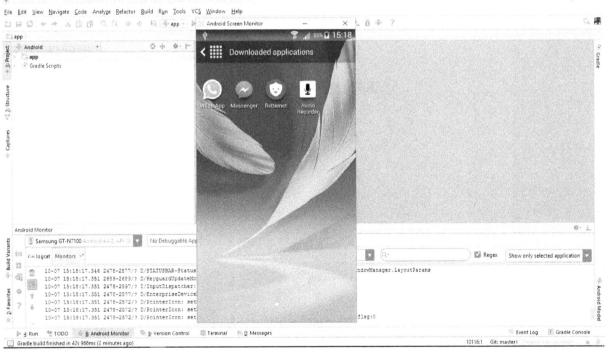

Fig. 5.36 | Audio Recorder Launcher Icon

Let us have a look at our Audio Recorder app from:
- Record Fig. 5.37.
- Stop Record Fig. 5.38.
- Play Fig. 5.39.

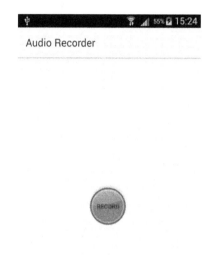

Fig. 5.37 | Record

Fig. 5.38 | Stop Record

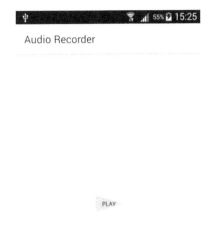

Fig. 5.39 | Play

- Stop Play Fig. 5.40.
- And back to Record (Same as Fig. 5.37)
- Saved Audio File Fig. 5.41.

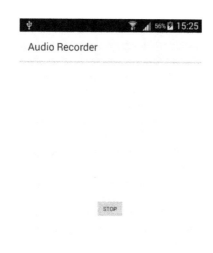

Fig. 5.40 | Stop Play

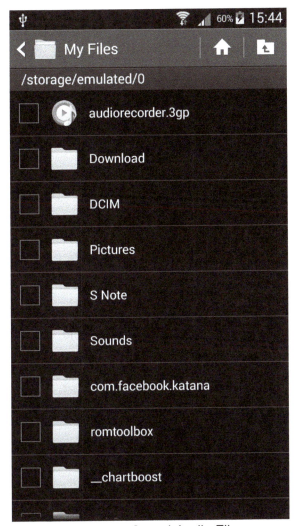

Fig. 5.41 | Saved Audio File

Code Inspection

There are a number of ways of inspecting the code, one way is by looking at your code but what if you have a huge application and thousands of line of code need to be inspected, there are other better ways that are already available by using the inbuilt tool Lint which can be run through the command line or Android Studio itself.

Configuring Lint

To set default Lint Checks Fig. 5.42:

- Select File > Other Settings > Default Settings.
- Select Editor > Inspections.
- In the Profile field, select Default or Project Default to set the scope for Android Studio or just for this project, respectively.
- Expand a category and change the Lint settings as needed.
- Click OK.

Running Lint

Lint tool checks your code while you are already using Android Studio. You can view warnings and errors in two ways:

- As pop-up text in the Code Editor. When Lint finds a problem, it highlights the problematic code in yellow or underlines the code in red for more serious issues
- In the Lint Inspection Results window after you select Analyze > Inspect Code as seen in Fig. 5.43 and Fig. 5.44.

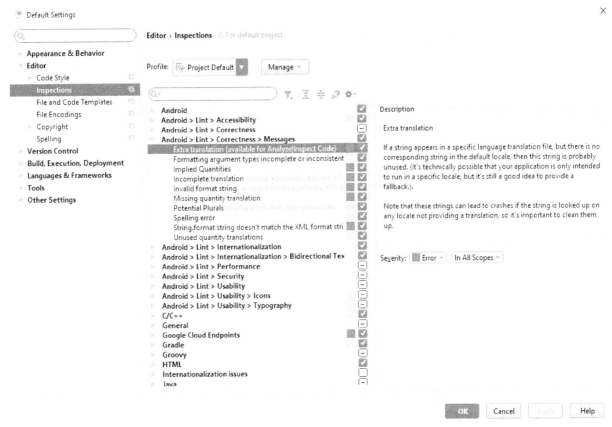

Fig. 5.42 | Configuring Lint

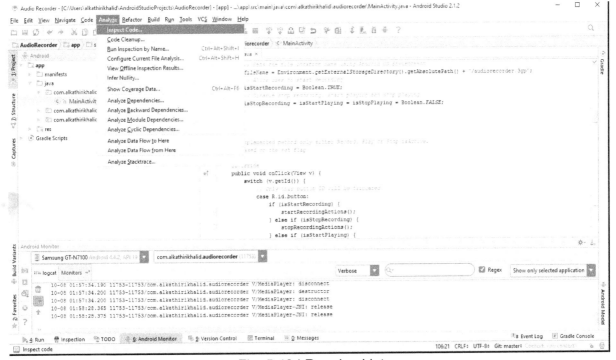

Fig. 5.43 | Running Lint

Lint Results

The inspection results will be shown with information such as name, location, result type and sometimes suggested solutions depending on the results as seen in Fig. 5.45

Further testing is also possible, Android makes it possible with just a few clicks, you can set up a JUnit test that runs on the local Java Virtual Machine (JVM) or an instrumented test that runs on a device.

You can also extend your testing by integrating test frameworks like Mockito to test Android API calls in your local unit tests, and Espresso or UI Automator to exercise user interaction in your instrumented tests.

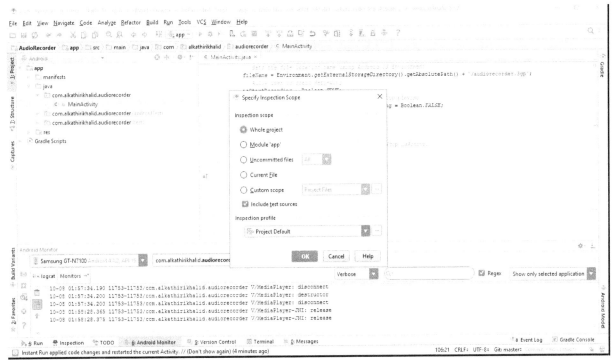

Fig. 5.44 | Whole project lint inspection

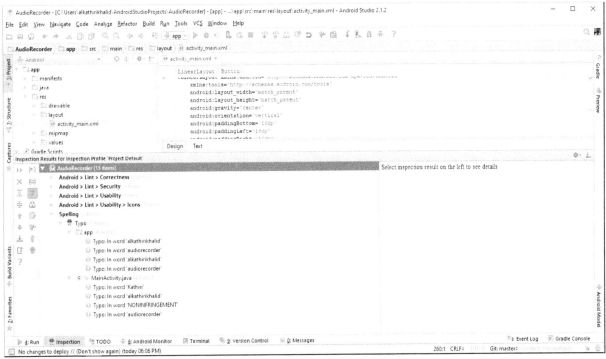

Fig. 5.45 | Lint inspection results

Knowledge Check

1. What do you understand by this line of code found in the manifest file android:theme="@style/Base.Theme.AppCompat.Light"
2. When and why would you use a FrameLayout rather than LinearLayout
3. Is it advisable and appropriate to use our own drawable resources or stick to the inbuilt from Android?
4. Does making all the string as a resource help in allowing your app to be easily translated to other languages?
5. Why would you implement an onClickListener rather than just create a new onClickListener?
6. A user has multiple buttons in his application and he has set them / bind them to an onClickListener, how would he differentiate and know where or which button was actually clicked?
7. The AudioRecorder app uses two classes from Android that allows it to Record and play audio, namely?
8. What would happen if you don't provide permission in the Manifest file for the AudioRecord App?
9. Is lint continuously checking your code while actively coding?
10. What are some of the exceptions you as a developer can anticipate while building AudioRecorder app?

Lab Exercise

After building the AudioRecorder app and setting up git as explained in the chapter, you may proceed with the lab, if any of the questions you answer yes, you may apply changes to your code.

1. Following good programming practices such as spacing and commenting, what other improvements can be done to the code?
   a. Is it important or vital for the code to be at a certain maximum length in a class i.e. 300 lines?
   b. Are there repetitive actions that can only have a single place to be called / referenced in AudioRecorder?
2. Is single responsibility applicable in AudioRecorder App?
3. Add a storage checker in your code to see if external storage is available for reading or writing and handle the application accordingly if not.
4. Add a way for the user to replay previous record/s in the AudioRecorder app.
5. Translate the Audio Recorder app to include your native language.

Chapter 6

Introduction

We have come to the end of the chapter and now it is time to publish our app to play store, there are however few things we need to do before publishing.

Prerelease Preparation

Basically publishing means two things
- Prepare your app for release: configure, build and test
- Release your app: publicize, sell and distribute

Here you will need to consider things like End User Agreement, Application Icon, choosing a good package name as a package is unique and cannot be changed and must be suitable over the life of the app, remove logging and disable debugging, remove stray or unused files in your project that can prevent the app from compiling and cause your app to behave unpredictably.

You will also need to add support for multiple screen configurations, optimize your app for Android tablet devices and also consider using the Support Library which provides static support libraries that you can add to your Android application, that allows you to use APIs that are either not available on older platform versions or use utility APIs that are not part of the framework APIs.

After building the app, if needed prepare secure servers if you are dealing with payments especially if you are implementing in app billing and performing signature verification on your server, if your app need to fetch real time data, make sure the data is up to date and the server can handle the load that you are expecting or anticipating and finally test your app.

Versioning and Upgrades

Android does not enforce restriction on versioning, as a developer you are responsible for this in order to allow smooth upgrade, downgrade or compatibility, versioning allows:
- Users to have specific information about the app on their devices and the upgrade available for them
- If you publish apps as a suite, the other apps need to query the system for the app's version, in order to determine compatibility or identify any dependencies
- A publishing service may also need to check the app version to determine compatibility and establish if a user needs to upgrade or downgrade

Fig. 6.1. Gradle Scripts > build.gradle (Module: app):
- android:versionCode increasing integer (2100000000 max)
- android:versionName human-readable string

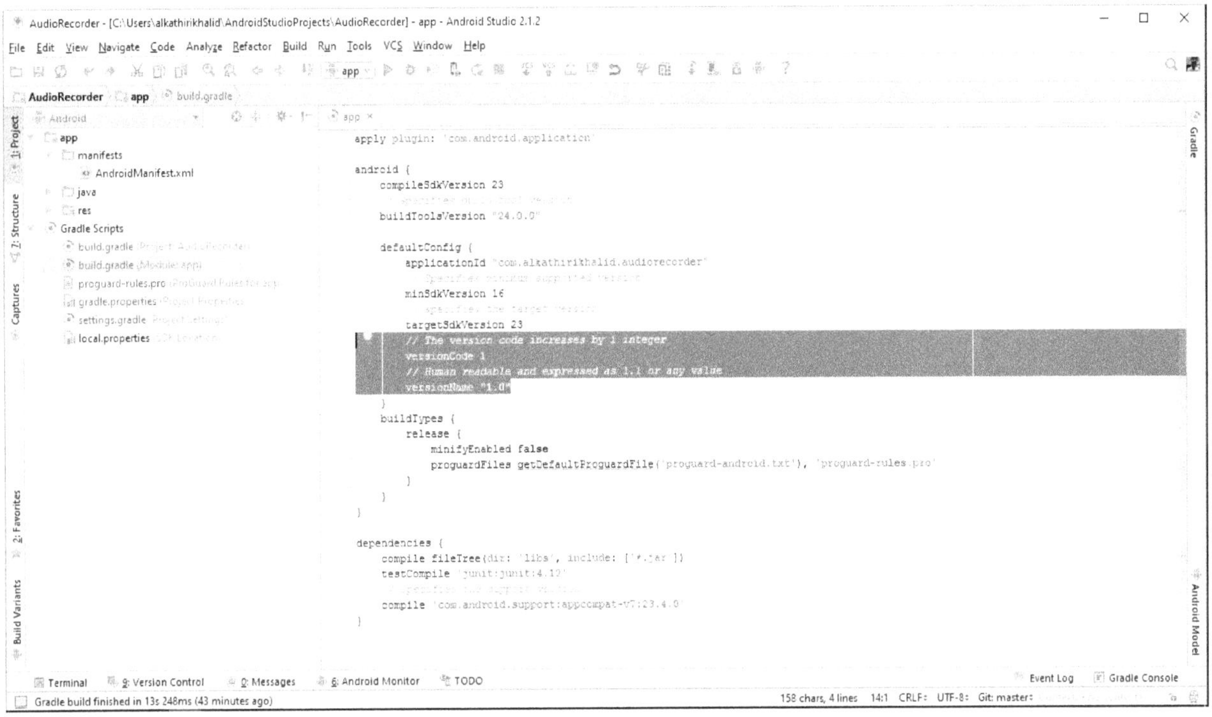

Fig. 6.1 | versionCode and versionName

Signing and Packaging to APK

All applications published to play store must be signed with a release KEY the key, when you sign an APK, the signing tool attaches the public-key certificate to the APK. The public-key certificate serves as a fingerprint that uniquely identifies the APK to you and your private key. This helps Android ensure that any future updates to your APK are authentic and come from the original author, the key can have a life time of up to 1000 years, you are encouraged to sign your application with a minimum of 25 yrs. and above.

By default, all development environment whenever you run or debug an app to a phone it gets sign with a debug key which has an expiration date of 365 days from its creation date, since the debug certificate is created by the build tools and is insecure than a release key, most app stores like Google Play Store will not accept an APK signed with a debug certificate key for publishing. The key resides in HomeDirectory/.android/debug.keystore as seen in Fig. 6.2.

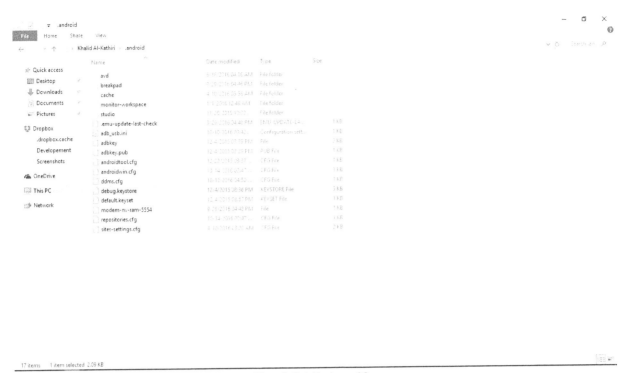

Fig. 6.2 | Debug Key

Creating Release Key and Signing a release build

As we have seen with debug key it gets generated automatically and once it expires, you just need to deleted from its directory and another one will automatically get generated when you debug an app.

There are two ways of generating a release key through:
- Android Studio
- Command Line

Through Android Studio

It uses Keytool, a java tool that allows you to sign or encrypt web sites, it's basically a Key and Certificate Management Tool, click:
- Build > Generate Signed APK

Within Keystore path, you may Create New or Choose Existing, since we are in the process of creating a release key choose New Fig. 6.3.

The wizard will remember your details on the next step on signing as seen in Fig. 6.4. In the event you are using and should be using this key for another app, make sure you remember your credentials, make sure build type is set as release and click Finish.

The other way through Android Studio is that you can also configure the Build process to automatically sign Your APK.

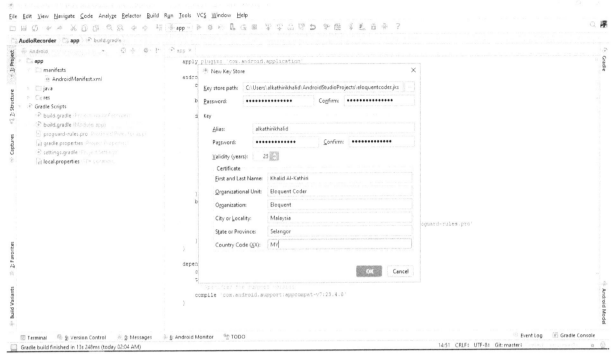

Fig. 6.3 | Creating a new Key

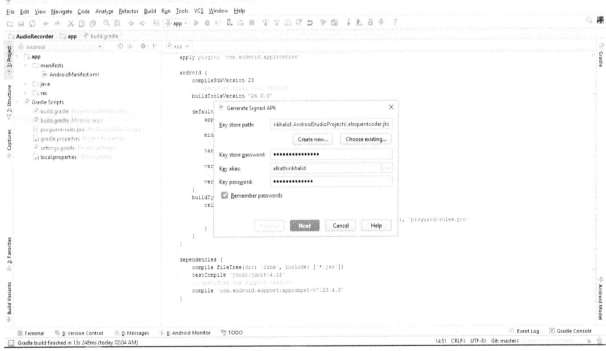

Fig. 6.4 | Signing an App using Key

Once the generation process is complete you will get a generated app-release.apk file in the destination folder you previously specified as depicted in Fig. 6.5.

Through Command line

Since we have already set up our path previously we can easily run Keytool Fig. 6.6.

```
keytool -genkey -v -keystore my-release-key.jks
```

It will take us to the same steps of setting up a password and personal details such as name and organization name as seen previously but now in command line.

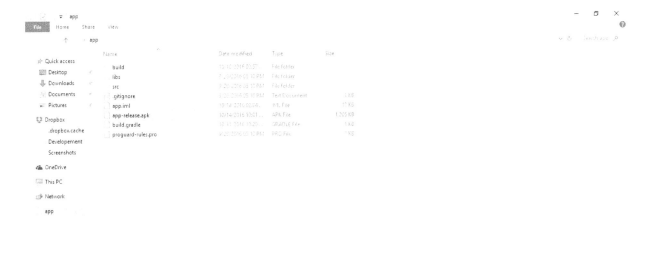

Fig. 6.5 | APK file generate

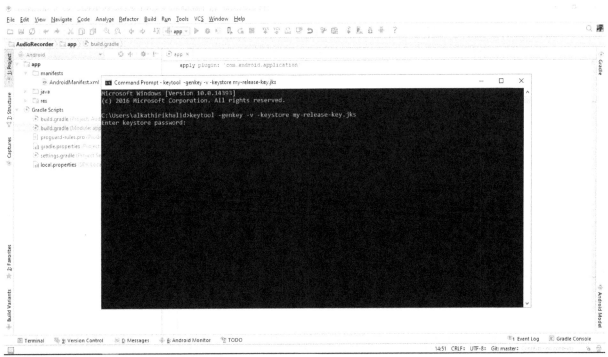

Fig. 6.6 | Key generation through command line

Google Play

Now we are ready to publish our app, we will need to sign up for a developer account and make a onetime payment, things to consider before jumping to signup are:

- Register for a Google Play publisher account
- Set up a Google Wallet Merchant Account in order to accept payment
- Your country of residence and if your country can sell app in Google Play

Sign Up for a Publisher Account

The first step is to visit the Google Play Developer Console and register for a publisher account.

- Visit the Google Play Developer Console at https://play.google.com/apps/publish/signup Fig. 6.7.
- Enter personal information about your developer or company identity, developer name or company name, email address. You can modify this information later
- Read and accept the Developer Distribution Agreement that applies to your country or region. Note that apps and store listings that you publish on Google Play must comply with the Developer Program Policies and US export law
- Pay a $25 USD registration fee using Google Wallet. If you do not have a Google Wallet account, you can quickly set one up during the process Fig. 6.8.

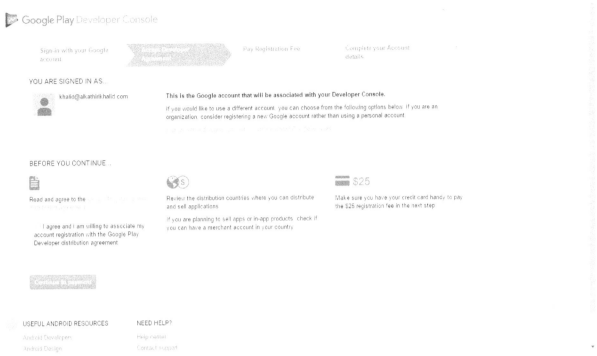

Fig. 6.7 | Developer Console Signup Process

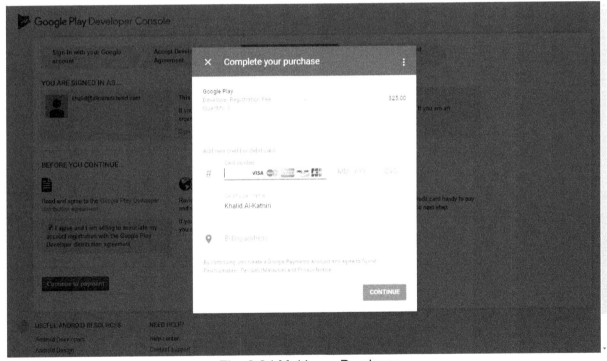

Fig. 6.8 | Making a Purchase

Merchant Countries

These are the supported countries for developers or companies to sell apps in Google Play, make sure your country is in the list so as to be in a position to sell and receive payments, there is a work around where if a supported country is a neighboring country and you interest such as a property or physical address and a bank account, you may proceed with those information, all countries have their laws, regulations and tax requirements.

You can get further information from the link below:

* https://support.google.com/googleplay/android-developer/table/3541286?hl=en

Fig. 6.9. Showing some of the supported countries in the above link.

Location	Download free apps	Download paid apps	Buyer Currency and Price Range
Albania	✓	✓	★
Algeria	✓	✓	★
Angola	✓	✓	★
Antigua and Barbuda	✓	✓	★
Argentina	✓	✓	★
Armenia	✓	✓	★
Aruba	✓	✓	★
Australia	✓	✓	AUD .99 - 550.00
Austria	✓	✓	EUR .50 - 350.00
Azerbaijan	✓	✓	★
Bahamas	✓	✓	★
Bahrain	✓	✓	USD .99 - 400.00
Bangladesh	✓	✓	★
Belarus	✓	✓	★
Belgium	✓	✓	EUR .50 - 350.00
Belize	✓	✓	★
Benin	✓	✓	★
Bolivia	✓	✓	BOB 7.00 - 2,800.00
Bosnia and Herzegovina	✓	✓	★
Botswana	✓	✓	★
Brazil	✓	✓	BRL 0.99 - 1,500.00
Bulgaria	✓	✓	BGN 1.50 - 700.00
Burkina Faso	✓	✓	★

Fig. 6.9 | Some of the Supported Merchant Countries

Merchant Account

If you want to sell products on Google Play priced apps, in-app products, or subscriptions you will also need to set up a Google Wallet Merchant Account. You can do that at any time, but make sure to first review the list of merchant countries.

To set up a Merchant account from the Developer Console Fig. 6.10:
- Sign in to your Google Play Developer Console at https://play.google.com/apps/publish/
- Open Financial reports on the side navigation
- Click Setup a Merchant Account now

If you have set up previously you will be able to get financial reports as seen in Fig. 6.11.

Remember:
- Since package name is unique, If the manifest package name has changed, the new application will be installed alongside the old application, so they both coexist on the user's device at the same time so make sure it is the same package name if it is an upgrade
- If the signing certificate changes, trying to install the new application onto the device will fail until the old version is uninstalled

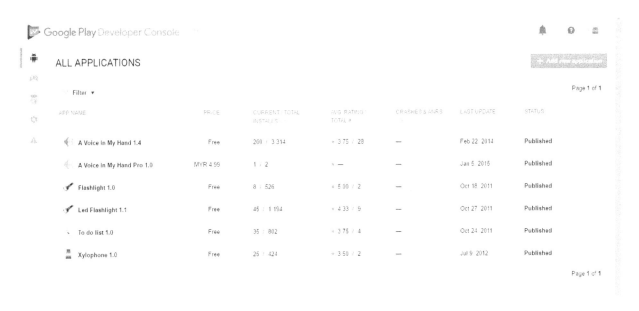

Fig. 6.10 | Developer Console

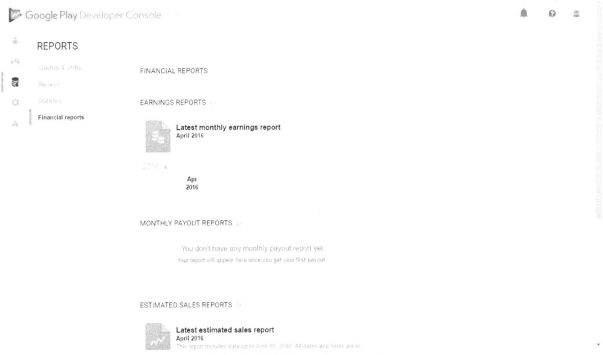

Fig. 6.11 | Financial Reports

Uploading APK file to Google Play

Within Developer console on the top right click "Add New Application" give it a title and you may choose to either as seen in Fig 6.12:

- Upload APK
- Prepare Store Listing

You may choose any, it will still take out to Prepare Store Listing for you to upload images for the app to be used in Google Play, and what the users will read and get what your app is all about, you will need to provide information about your application and screen shots, translations and including privacy policy as seen in Fig. 6.13.

Follow the wizard step by step for a successful upload and publishing and fix any errors and add all mandatory information and images.

Once all that is done Google Play will notify you when your app will be available and you will be able to see it not only in your developer console but also in play store, when you search uniquely be its package name i.e. 'com.alkathirikhalid', as the probability of other apps with the same name as yours already exists, or search by publisher name such as 'pub:Al-Kathiri Khalid'.

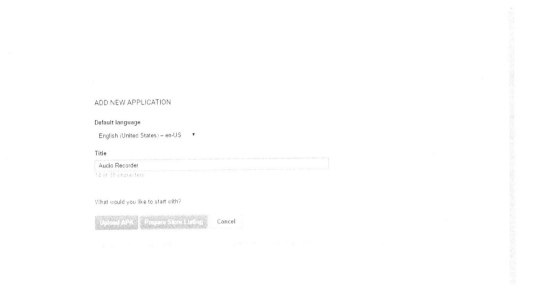

Fig. 6.12 | Giving a Title

Fig. 6.13 | Fill required details and upload screen shots

Distribution

You are not restricted or restrained to only upload, distribute or sell apps in Google Play.

Through Other Markets

You could alternatively market your application in other places for maximum reach and profit such as:
- Amazon App Store
- Mobogenie
- SlideME
- Opera Mobile Store
- etc.

See Fig. 6.14. Make sure you understand the terms, conditions and payment fee or percentage earning fee if any.

Through Email

You could also simply email your application to trusted individuals, Android will detect the apk file and ask for your permission to install, only if a user has configured their device to allow installation from unknown sources Fig. 6.15. and has opened your email with the Gmail.

This would not protect you from individuals who could reverse engineer your app by extracting your apk file and using decompilers to access source code or simply unauthorized redistribution from the intended first recipient. You could make an internal checking to verify the app is running in a given device or the intended user by reading the device unique data such as the email for Google Account, SIM number etc. this will require you to get prior consent from your clients.

Through Website link

You could allow the user to navigate and download your application, Android will detect the apk file and ask for your permission to install again only if a user has configured their device to allow installation from unknown sources.

This has the same risks as through email as you are exposing your apk file.

TIP #24: If distributing through APK is unavoidable you could code your application to only accept certain devices by knowing the devices the app will run on in advance or you could enable ProGuard which obfuscates classes, fields, and methods with short names hence making your APK difficult to reverse engineer.

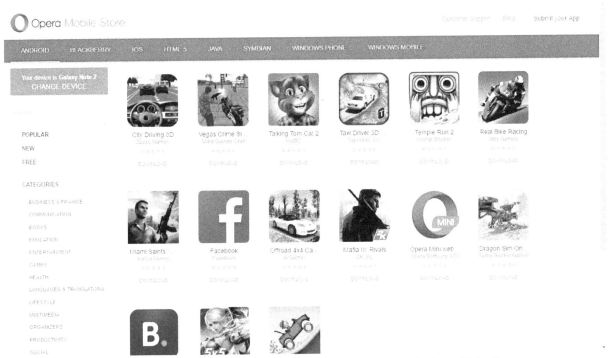

Fig. 6.14 | Opera Mobile Store Selected Device Galaxy Note 2

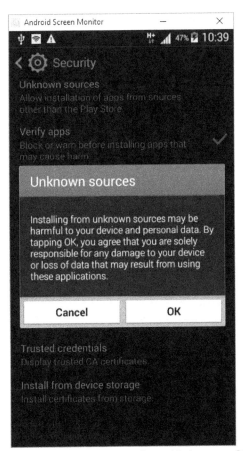

Fig. 6.15 | Allow Installation from Unknown Sources

Knowledge Check

1. Explain android:VersionCode
2. Explain android:VersionName
3. What is the recommended minimum life of your release key?
4. How about the maximum life of a release key?
5. A developer notices that the debug key has expired, how can he fix this?
6. Is a must to have a release key to distribute to Play Store or Other Stores?
7. Keytool is a java tool, True/ False?
8. What is the amount a developer needs to pay to start publishing in Play Store?
9. Explain Merchant Countries and Merchant Account.
10. Explain Google Wallet and how it is applicable to publishing an App?

Lab Exercise

The whole lab activity is optional but highly recommended as it involves signup and payment.

1. Create a Release Key
2. Sign your AudioRecorder or an App of your choice that you own with your Release key
   a. Ensure version come and version name are correct and appropriate
   b. Ensure package name is unique
3. Signup for an Android Publisher Account
   a. Ensure your country is within Merchant countries list if you wish to sell and receive money for your sells
4. Upload your APK file
5. Add resources to your App in play store such as screenshots, end user agreement, follow the online wizard for best recommendation.

Index

A

Account, 206, 210, 214, 216, 217
adb, 30, 38, 41, 42, 54
APIs, 14, 70, 72, 73, 198
APK, 200, 202, 205, 212, 214, 217
AVD, 23, 32, 33, 34, 36, 38, 41, 44, 45, 54, 58, 81, 152, 186

C

channel, 26
Chart, 14, 47, 48
Code completion, 40
Command, 33, 41, 42, 52, 54, 57, 80, 84, 100, 202, 204

D

dashboards, 14
Driver, 28, 38, 39

E

Environment, 14, 18, 21, 48, 88, 100, 162, 163

F

Froyo, 46

G

Git, 14, 26, 82, 84, 85, 86, 87, 88, 89, 96, 97, 98, 100, 102, 112, 114, 115, 124, 128, 129, 130, 154, 167

GitHub, 14, 26, 82, 96
GPU, 36

H

HAXM, 23, 28, 34, 36

I

Installation, 16, 22, 23, 25, 32, 40, 84, 85, 215

J

javac, 16, 18, 22
JAVASE, 18
JDK, 16, 18, 19, 21, 22
JetBrains', 21

K

keymap, 40
KitKat, 36, 80

L

launch, 22, 24, 28, 34, 36, 46, 64, 156, 159, 186
Lollipop, 14, 21, 36

M

Manager, 21, 28, 32, 33, 34, 36, 41, 45, 70, 73
Merchant, 206, 208, 209, 210, 216, 217

N

Nexus, 32, 34, 36, 38

O

OEM, 38
OOP, 15, 16

P

Path, 18, 19, 22, 30, 31, 32, 41, 52, 87, 162
Play Store, 14, 48, 54, 146, 148, 200, 216

R

Reformat code, 40
Repository, 28
Requirements, 21

S

SDK, 14, 21, 22, 23, 28, 29, 30, 31, 32, 40, 41, 44, 45, 46, 48, 52, 90, 148
Settings, 26, 27, 34, 37, 38, 73, 88, 192
Setup, 18, 22, 30, 31, 32, 34, 38, 40, 41, 45, 52, 54, 85, 88, 89, 96, 113, 210

V

VersionCode, 216
VersionName, 216
Virtual Device, 32, 34, 36, 42, 54